PREHISTORIC
NORTHUMBERLAND

PREHISTORIC
NORTHUMBERLAND

Stan Beckensall

TEMPUS

First published 2003
Reprinted 2006

Tempus Publishing Limited
The Mill, Brimscombe Port,
Stroud, Gloucestershire, GL5 2QG
www.tempus-publishing.com

British Library Cataloguing in Publication Data.
A catalogue record for this book is available from the British Library.

ISBN 0 7524 2543 9

Typesetting and origination by Tempus Publishing Limited.
Printed in Great Britain.

CONTENTS

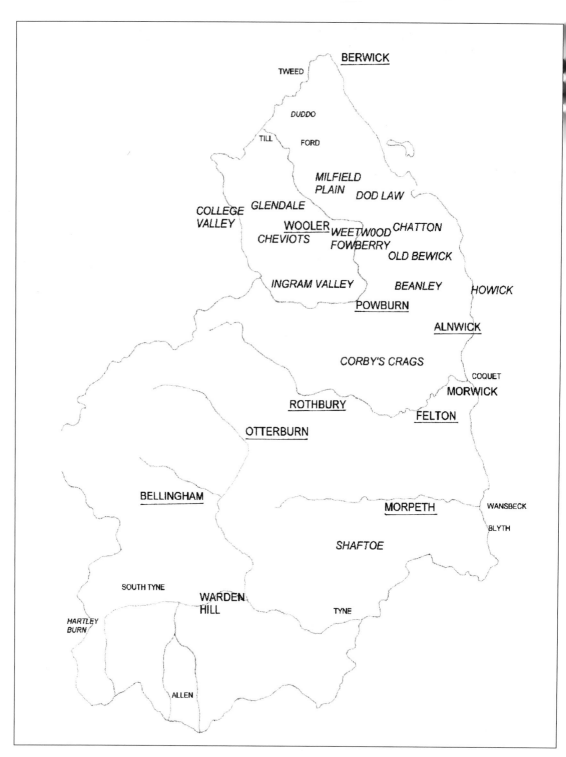

1 *Northumberland, with some selected sites. Underlined places give a general guide to locations over a large area*

ACKNOWLEDGEMENTS

Although I have been able to include my own original contributions to the archaeology of Northumberland, the writing of this book would have been impossible without reference to the work of so many others. Northumberland is, fortunately, an area where professional and independent archaeologists have found it easy to work together. Without this symbiosis much of the work of excavation and fieldwork would not have happened. The Northumberland Archaeological Group, for example, with its leadership of professional archaeologists such as Professor George Jobey, Colin Burgess, Keith Blood, Roger Miket and Peter Topping, has made a long-standing contribution to prehistoric exploration through fieldwork and excavation. Their work is apparent in the text, the basis of illustrations, and in the bibliography. As my excavations and theirs show, the involvement of non-professional archaeologists brings to an excavation a wealth of other experience and enthusiasm that is heart-warming. Dr Clive Waddington is one of the new generation of archaeologists to continue this tradition with great vigour and skill.

I have found the text more difficult to write than a more limited topic; it is aimed at different audiences, and it is difficult to satisfy both the professional archaeologist and people who know little about the subject. I hope that the compromise will be helped by the illustrations. Most of these are my own, but where they are either based on others' work or on their photographs, this has been acknowledged in the text. I am grateful to Lindsay Allason-Jones, Director of the Museum of Antiquities of the University and Society of Antiquities of Newcastle upon Tyne for access to their material (NUM), including air photographs by Professor Norman McCord. Some photographs and drawings are repeated from my previous work; I again thank Cambridge University, the British Museum and Birtley Aris.

Naturally, I take full responsibility for the text. Sometimes I have had to speculate about the significance of current excavations that I have experienced before the final reports have been produced; these can only be interim remarks. I am grateful to Professor Richard Bradley (Reading University), and Caroline Hardie (Northumberland archaeologist and joint Conservation Team Manager) for reading a draft of the script and for their comments. Paul Frodsham, who has written the Foreword, and Peter Carne (Field Officer of Archaeological Services at Durham University) have for years been unstinting with their help. Paul's advice on the text has been outstandingly valuable, and has prevented many errors from slipping through. In Hexham, Matthew Hutchinson and Anna Rossiter have ensured that what I write should be for a wide audience.

I am grateful to Ian and Irene Hewitt for sharing my work at Blawearie and in rock art and for allowing me to use their illustrations, and to Paul Brown for his maps of rock art sites and Old Bewick.

I should like to thank especially Fritz Berthele for his unique contribution to prehistory through years of fieldwalking: his collection is outstanding.

I thank the pilot Jim Martin and the Felton/Eshott microlight pilots who have shared my enthusiasm and enabled me to take aerial photographs.

Finally, the covers of all my books have provided so many people with great pleasure, for the artwork is original and potent. Again, I thank Gordon Highmoor for this, and for the frontispiece.

FOREWORD

Paul Frodsham
Archaeologist, Northumberland National Park Authority

Northumberland is traversed by one of the most spectacular ancient monuments in the world, Hadrian's Wall, built in the years following AD 122 'to separate the Romans from the barbarians'. After the Romans, the ever fluctuating boundaries of the shadowy Dark Age British confederacies and the Anglian Kingdom of Northumbria, and the ever present threat of conflict with neighbouring kingdoms, ensured that the expansion and defence of boundaries remained of paramount importance to those in power. In medieval times, Northumberland found itself as the northernmost territory within the kingdom of England, and the numerous castles, towers and bastle houses so beloved of today's tourists bear stark witness to the five-and-a-bit centuries of intermittent conflict between England and Scotland prior to the Union of the Crowns in 1603. Thus it will be readily appreciated that much of the history of Northumberland is intimately linked to the region's status as a frontier zone.

With so much of its archaeology arising out of its position 'on the edge', it often comes as something of a surprise for people to realise that Northumberland actually represents the heart of Britain, and that some 400 or more generations of 'prehistoric' people had lived and died here before Hadrian dreamed up his Wall. The often spectacular archaeological remains associated with the Roman and the Anglo-Scottish borders have tended to grab the attention of locals and visitors alike, but many of Northumberland's fascinating prehistoric monuments are no less dramatic and indeed are considered by a minority of archaeologists (of whom Stan and I are perhaps two of the most vocal!) to be altogether more interesting.

In fact the prehistoric landscapes of upland Northumberland are second to none, and in future they are destined to become much more widely understood and appreciated. In comparison to other regions of Britain, they have been relatively little studied since the pioneering work of George Tate and Henry MacLaughlan in the mid-nineteenth century, but this is not necessarily bad news as it means there is still an enormous amount of exciting work to be done, much of which can employ techniques unavailable to earlier generations. Some

2 *Stan's work spans the divide between popular archaeology and academia. An increasing amount of serious academic study is now being based on his initial studies into rock art. Professor Richard Bradley was the first academic to realise the potential of Stan's work, and much important research has resulted from collaboration between the two. Here Stan, resplendent in hand-knitted rock art jumper, is seen with Richard in 1992 during a visit to the extraordinary rock carvings at Morwick Mill near Warkworth*

of this work is already underway, with present day archaeologists such as Peter Topping and Clive Waddington doing much to build on the earlier efforts of George Jobey, Colin Burgess and Roger Miket, to name but three.

The relative lack of research over the past 150 years is in large part due to our distance from the decision makers and budget holders in London (our 'distant' location at the edge of England continues to exert a negative influence on some things even today), but is also due in no small part to the lack of a University archaeology department in the 'void' between Newcastle and Edinburgh. Having spent the last decade of my life working in this 'void' I am constantly frustrated by members of the public asking where they can obtain a book about local prehistory and having to tell them that they can't. My excuse has been that all professional archaeologists in the region are too busy with mundane everyday work to entertain the exciting notion of writing a book, but now, thanks to Stan Beckensall, things have changed for the better.

I well remember the first time I met Stan. It was on a typically grey and wet Northumbrian morning at Easter 1992, in a layby on the A697 near Snook Bank. We had descended on the area due to our shared enthusiasm for (some would say obsession with) prehistoric rock art. I had been aware of Stan's work on rock art for some time, but to meet him was indeed an experience. Within no time at all I was aware of the passion for the Northumberland landscape that burns in his heart, and this passion, coupled with his encyclopaedic knowledge of local rock art borne of decades of personal research in the wild hills, was to draw me into a friendship as valuable as any I have made during my time here.

I recall sitting in Stan's study several years ago urging him to find a publisher who would place his work in front of a wider audience through quality publications: thanks to Tempus this is now happening and Stan is receiving the plaudits that his work deserves. Visits to Stan's study are rarely less than inspirational. If we ever tire of talking about rock art then his dear wife Jane's arguably slightly less eccentric hobby of tortoise breeding always provides fascinating relief, though I have to say that we only rarely get around to having a look at the tortoises. I remember arriving on one occasion to find a full-scale 'replica' of the Barcloddiad y Gawres chambered tomb, formed by rubbings of the decorated stones draped over various items of furniture. Stan had spent a week on Anglesey, and had, of course, come home with rubbings of all the rock art that he had encountered on his travels. Such work adds to the phenomenal record of local rock art that Stan has accumulated over the years, and it is to his immense credit that he is currently liaising with the University of Newcastle to ensure that all this material is properly sorted, archived, and made available to the public over the internet.

Stan will always be best known for his work on rock art but, as is clear from this book, his remit extends much wider. While most professional archaeologists in Northumberland have found themselves engaged in important but largely routine tasks over recent years, Stan, unburdened by the constraints of such office, has contributed to numerous initiatives aimed at furthering our understanding of local prehistory. He has done this on two levels: first, by making countless new discoveries and contributing details of these to the county Sites and Monuments Record; second, and no less importantly, he has undertaken an enormous amount of work in presenting information about prehistory at a popular level to local people. On several occasions, while discussing one site or another at one of my own evening presentations at some far flung pub or village hall, a voice has piped up from somewhere – 'we know all about that: Mr Beckensall told us about it years ago!' I would hazard a guess that Stan

3 *Stan gave of his time voluntarily to contribute to the Northumberland National Park/University of Durham 'Breamish Valley Archaeology Project'. Here he is seen with student Janet Beveridge after discovering a 4,000-year-old Early Bronze Age Food Vessel in a burial cairn at Ingram. Stan's enthusiasm and sheer delight at the discovery are clear for all to see!*

has probably given more public lectures about local archaeology over the past 30 years than anyone else, and this book provides a welcome opportunity for him to present his views to an even wider audience.

In addition to his passion for prehistoric archaeology, Stan is also a talented playwright, poet and photographer: a number of his own air photographs, most taken while hanging precariously out of a microlite, are effectively used to help illustrate this book. Above everything, however, he is a loving family man. How he ever finds the time to fit his archaeology in alongside everything else I will never know, but everyone interested in Northumberland's prehistory should be grateful that he does. In this book he presents the results of some of his own research alongside the work of others (including discussion of published reports and recent and current projects which will not be officially published for several years) to provide the first ever quality book dedicated to the fabulous prehistory of this most magnificent of English counties.

One of the joys of writing about prehistory is that there are so many different ways of going about it, none of which are necessarily right or wrong. I could legitimately take issue with some of the detail in Stan's text, or indeed question the basic structure of the book, but Stan has earned the right to present his own angle on local prehistory, and I have no doubt that his approach will prove exceedingly popular amongst native Northumbrians and others with an interest in the region. In the fullness of time, there will no doubt be many other quality books about prehistoric Northumberland. As I write I am aware of a number of others that are in preparation, and there is every chance that the next couple of decades could prove to be something of a golden age for local prehistory, which may at last begin to emerge from beneath the shadow of that Wall. Regardless of the number of popular overviews of Northumberland's prehistory that appear in the future, however, it will never surprise those of us fortunate enough to know him that it is Stan who has written the first!

I have described Stan elsewhere as Northumberland's 'last great gentleman antiquarian'. This is peculiarly appropriate for someone who has laboured so long and so hard, often in splendid isolation, without financial reward, in an archaeological world dominated by 'professional' rules and regulations. All professional archaeologists hoping to work in Northumberland will now be duty bound to read this book, and if they think they can improve on it then they should attempt to do so. If not, then they should thank Stan for this contribution before disappearing back down their grubby holes or retreating into their comfortable ivory towers to concentrate on their own important, and often very specialised, contributions to the study of local prehistory. We can be certain that the often unheralded efforts of various such specialists will contribute in due course to a much revised understanding of Northumberland's prehistory. For now, however, this book is a welcome attempt to provide a synthesis that has been demanded by the Northumbrian public for several years. That public will not be disappointed by its content.

1

NORTHUMBERLAND LANDSCAPE

It is difficult to imagine what the landscape was like in prehistory. We know that there are some unalterable features: the main solid geology that underlies our land. Features such as hills and scarps have been with us for millions of years; some of the soils are much more recent, brought down by ice and water when other rocks have been eroded. Rivers change direction. The east coast is slowly subsiding into the sea.

The underlying rocks, height above sea level, soil deposits, climate and microclimate (special local conditions) determine what will grow on the land. People can change the vegetation cover by removing woodland with axe and fire, by encouraging the growth of some plants at the expense of others, by ploughing, sowing crops or by grazing animals. They can also break away some of the solid rock with mining and quarrying. These are very important changes, but if we try to put ourselves back mentally into a pristine wilderness before the more significant changes occurred we will realise that there were outstanding features that acted not only as guides through the country but also as foci for scattered people to meet. Hunting groups, for example, might go in different directions and be able to find their way back to common meeting places marked by natural features. These 'natural places' may remain unaltered in one sense, but may change according to the way that people attach significance to them, seen through 'the eye of the beholder'. We may see a rock overhang as a place to sit and look at a view; to others it may have been the entrance into an underground spirit world, a vital place to rest temporarily to sort out the weapons of hunting, or a place that marks the beginning of someone else's territory. It could have been a place where the ancestors dwelt. What may be for us an easy stroll to reach may have been fraught with peril.

We may not realise that a natural feature or small part of an area such as a waterfall might have appeared in the past as a place of magic, myth or legend. Dependence on outside forces and fear may have led people to search for help; that help may have been thought of as inherent in certain special places. We may become so familiar with our landscape that a sense of awe and wonder

4 Natural shapes in dolerite at Dunstanburgh Castle

may disappear. For prehistoric people an individual tree, spring, animal or bird could become an object of veneration, imbued with some mystical power. Omens might abound; this is not surprising when we see in our own society a belief in horoscopes or in throwing salt over one's shoulder.

We can think about how this might work in the past. Places like Shaftoe Crags (**colour plate 4**) have rock formations that stand out: there is unusual architecture in a natural small cavern, and the profile of a bearded man. At Dunstanburgh (**4**) the columnar basalt has eroded into statues rather like those on Easter Island. Fluted sandstone cliffs rise to the sky. Rounded hills wear a cap of cloud. The sea thunders in through a gap in the rocks, sending up spray. The outstanding, unusual profile of Simonside, a hill seen from so many places in Northumberland, is such a powerful visual presence in the landscape that Paul Frodsham (2000 and 2003 forthcoming) considers it likely to have been regarded as a 'sacred mountain' from prehistoric times onwards, although its significance may have changed. It could have been to central Northumberland what Ayers Rock was, and still is, to the Australian aborigines.

Even today we can sense what I have called 'The Power of Place' (Beckensall 2001). We have a cool web of language to protect us from fear until something so dramatic happens that our upbringing cannot help us cope with the reality of catastrophe. We wear our civilised clothes over naked bodies.

Natural places may also be resources. A particular type of rock may be of enormous value: something from which people can make good axes, blades, scrapers and points. If the material is rare, the place itself may take on a special significance and awe. Jet from Whitby, amber from the coast, with their curious electricity, lovely colours and texture, or a trapped insect within a stone, were exotic and desirable. Their sources may be protected and exploited by one group that sees the advantages of trading such rarities.

The land provided other resources; heavy soils did not drain well, but the swamps that they formed may have encouraged birds and animals that were hunted as food. Scarps with thin soils high above valleys provided easier places to move, to hunt, to pasture animals. Rivers were crossed in small boats or used to penetrate deeper into the land. Gravel plains with their well-drained soil became the easiest and most rewarding places to plough. Once the richness of an area was established, it might have been regarded as a gift to be cherished and protected. The land itself may have been venerated, worshipped for what it provided.

As the land was used more and opened up to a larger population, natural features come to mark areas that may be recognised as territories so that people do not clash. A place may have signalled the inherent right of people to be there. To these natural places and other signs of ownership may be added those that are deliberately created as monuments. Signs were left so that there was no mistake; they were there to jog people's memories. A natural place itself became a monument; the cliff at Morwick (**colour plate 1**) is a good example, for here a vertical outcrop of reddish rock close to the sea at a fording place has been covered with an astonishing variety of spirals. Not only would the river be full of fish, but it was also a main access to the hinterland from the sea in one of the most important river valleys in the county.

Upstanding features such as cliffs may have needed no further work on them to establish their importance as markers, but standing stones were erected to produce a satisfying sense of height and enclosure. Rock shelters, already prominent, were in at least five cases given additional status through rock art or used for burials.

History is about how people have used the landscape in which they found themselves to survive, to produce a surplus, and to ensure 'the survival of the tribe'. In different climates and with different geological structures and resources people adapt differently. The land is to be used, but it is to be respected. Changes in weather, the death of animals and the death of people are reminders that they are not in sole charge of their destinies, but they go on from day to day working to a future. What then did Northumberland offer to its early people?

In the north-west are the Cheviot Hills, like a crumpled upturned bowl with the Cheviot itself as the highest, rather flat summit. There is a core of granite with surrounding andesite, the result of long-expired volcanic activity. Moving east, south and south-east we come to the main rocks of the county, sedimentary sandstone, limestone, cementstone, millstone grit, coal and clays.

5 *From Humbleton Hill to Wooler and Ros Castle*

Pushing through in ridges are the molten sills of dolerite, or Whinstone, hard compact material favoured today as tough road metal. We see it in the central section of Hadrian's Wall or holding firmly the foundations of Bamburgh Castle. Along the faults, scarps of Fell sandstone are particularly prominent. Ice ages have swept tonnes of boulder clay across the solid rocks and gravel-filled basins. Rivers have deposited terraces of sands and gravels. There is a variety of soils, varying heights above sea level, and local microclimates. What grows is determined by a combination of all these features and by the intervention of people. As we tour the county we are aware of the great sweep of the lower lands of the coastal plain, which in the south-east has been the focus of modern industry because of the coal deposits that fuelled the Industrial Revolution. There are wide, extensive stretches of limestone and sandstone moorland rolling east from the flanks of the Pennines. There are no major dramatic mountain chains, but more subtle rises and falls in the land. The rounded Cheviots pour their streams east to the sea, while the Fell sandstone scarps run across the earth from north to south, swinging round to the south-west to form the Simonside Hills.

What we see today, the intensive arable cultivation in valleys, basins and coasts, is the product of hundreds of years of change and use. The Cheviots and scarps are now mainly used as pasture, but have not always been so: parts of the Cheviots are covered with terraces and rig and furrow systems of ploughing that speak of grain yields. They are now 'fossilised' by the growth of grass that has not been ploughed since. There are planted forests, some very large in extent. The Kielder reservoir drowned many early settlements. 'Natural' woodland only exists when it has been allowed to regenerate for centuries, and is now limited mainly to river valleys and moorland burns, where access for agriculture has been difficult. What woodland we do see is mostly planted recently. We may recover pictures of what the vegetation looked like in prehistoric times from sealed-in pollen deposits, and this pollen and tiny organisms may point to a picture of the climate at the time. This also enables us to assess what people were doing to the land.

An example of where pollen analysis has been used to reconstruct the landscape is on the coastal strip of Low Hauxley, south of Amble, from Mesolithic times to the present day, a period of over 8,000 years. What today is treeless and dune-covered was once tree-covered. The sand dunes were not formed until the Iron Age, about 3,000 years ago.

6 *Caller Crags: a Fell sandstone landscape*

This kind of information helps us to try and understand what sort of conditions our ancestors lived in at any time. All communities require basic food, water, clothing and shelter; we are interested in how they survived. We look also for surpluses, for trade, at the way in which power is based on acquiring things and how hierarchies formed.

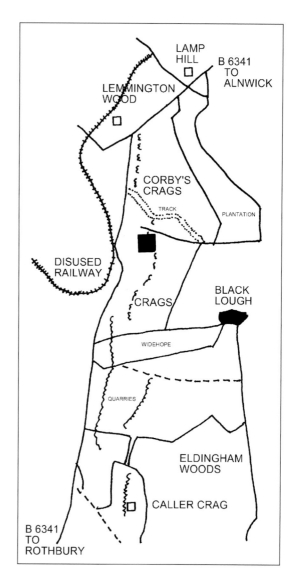

7 *Corby's Crags: the position of the rock shelter and enclosure are marked as a large black square. Other rock art sites are marked with small squares*

2

LAYERS OF TIME
HOW ARCHAEOLOGISTS WORK

We now move from the seen to what is hidden. Very often a site that is important for one generation or era remains important to other people, though perhaps in different ways. We may then find that time is marked in deposited layers; when they are excavated we may find evidence for the uses of the site in these layers. A good example is at Corby's Crags (NU 1279 0962).

Visible from the Alnwick-Rothbury road that runs past Edlingham church, castle and viaduct is a long oblique slit of a natural rock shelter beneath a dome of sandstone on the horizon. It is not the highest part of the range, which rises to a hill that has some boulders that look as though they might have belonged to a disturbed monument such as a stone circle. The dome has one of the finest viewpoints in the area, with Thrunton Crags and the Cheviot Hills visible. Below it towards the road, on a sloping platform, there is an enclosure, possibly Iron Age, with two concentric walls that end at the cliff edge above a small waterfall.

This is the edge of the Fell Sandstone scarp, where a fault line has caused the land to drop away to the north-west. Today it is rough moorland with the sunken circular depressions of old bell pits, used in more recent times for the small-scale extraction of coal. There are patches of coarse grass and bracken, with occasional stone quarries. There are other outcrops, less obvious than the dome of Corby's Crags, that may also have hollows beneath them. We tend to think that such things have been carefully examined, but this is not so. It is only recently that three runes (letters of the earliest Germanic alphabet) were discovered on outcrop rock at Lemmington Wood (NU 1294 1080) behind Ross Cottages, on the same outcrop as prehistoric rock art. There are also some small, unrecorded single standing stones on the moorland away from the scarp edge. The rock shelter itself and the nearby supposed Iron Age enclosure are recent discoveries; this shows the potential of the area for further investigation.

To summarise the site: the top of the dome has been cut into to provide a boundary between Percy and Swinburne lands (marked P/S on the rock) that continues down the rock in a series of cut steps. The boundary continues in the opposite direction as a wire fence. The domed outcrop has been partially

8 *Corby's Crags: the rock shelter is below the cleared field, the enclosure partly covered with scrub. To the left of the fence are bell pits*

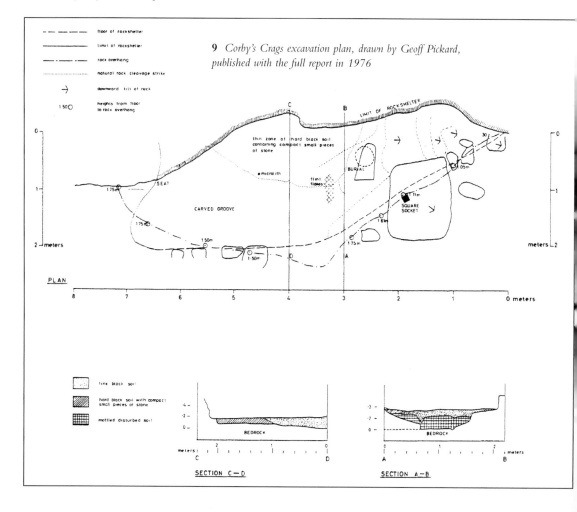

9 *Corby's Crags excavation plan, drawn by Geoff Pickard, published with the full report in 1976*

10 *The shelter floor: the pot was covered by the triangular stone. A pecked groove lies to the right of the pole*

quarried, with signs of millstone extraction, and this has confused the identification of what may be cup marks. However, there is a basin from which a groove runs down the dome at the centre of a ring. There are two standing stones on the slope below the overhang. On the floor of the rock shelter there was a mixture of artefacts from Middle Stone Age flint knapping (*c.*8000 years ago) to fragments of modern glass, clay pipes, a teacup and a penknife. This place had sheltered many people; recently an armchair and ledges cut into solid rock with metal tools made it a good place to sit, with part of the open end screened off. There are clear similarities between the use of this rock shelter and Goatscrag Hill (see below).

On the floor is a groove pecked with a hard stone tool leading to a triangular stone that covered a cremation burial in a Food Vessel of *c.*2000 BC. Although it is not possible to be categorical about this, there is likely to be a link between the pick marks on the floor and the basin and groove above. The vessel had been sunk into a pit in the floor, a slab placed over it, and the whole thing covered with soil that effectively hid it until the site was disturbed. As the base of the upright pot had suffered through the pit acting as a sump for water in the overhang, the whole pot and surrounding earth were removed for excavation. It is safe to say that no matter what the time-span may be, the place was of great significance to the makers of the motifs and those who buried the cremated remains of one of their people under the rock floor with a flat stone on top. A stray find nearby of a barbed and tanged arrowhead links it to the pot.

I excavated the floor of the shelter and the standing stone 5m away on the slope; the latter proved to have been erected not in a pit, but by wedging its wide flat base with stones to prevent it from toppling over. A definite link between the time the stone was erected and the prehistoric use of the shelter cannot be made, but is likely.

For many antiquarians from the past two centuries the actual artefacts (tools, pottery, jewellery, for example) used to be the most interesting things about an excavation, but for the archaeologist today *where* these objects are found is crucial to our understanding. The base of the shelter is solid sandstone. The pot was from a shallow pit dug into the floor of the overhang, but the disturbance of the accumulated soil on the floor revealed small pieces of flint that were left there by earlier hunter-gatherers who used the shelter temporarily to knap flint to make their hunting tools. This time is called *Mesolithic*, or Middle Stone Age (from the Greek lithos = stone, and meso = middle). A characteristic of these early people is the thin blades that they knapped, worked along the edge, and called *microliths* (meaning 'small stones'). We know this not from carbon dating this site, but from the form of the flints, which are like those found on many other Mesolithic sites throughout Britain. It is not always necessary to go to the expense of carbon dating if the date of an artefact is known. In addition to recognisable artefacts, the production of any flint implement on the spot may leave small pieces discarded or lost in making them from a larger piece of stone. There is more about the people who made these flints further on in the book.

Archaeologists examine layers in the soil from the earliest to latest times; sometimes the build up is disturbed. For example, if a farmer dug a deep pit through such layers to bury a dead animal, that animal would be at the bottom of the layers, not as the earliest event but as the latest. A pit would show in the layers.

The time when Mesolithic people used this early rock shelter was followed thousands of years later by its use in the early Bronze Age. The Bronze Age is a period that covers roughly 2100-700 BC. The early (or 'earlier') Bronze Age is a time when metals were introduced, but where people still made most of their tools from stone. As you will see further in the book, Bronze Age people are recognised particularly by their own types of pottery and by the way they buried their dead.

The feature that drew my attention to the rock shelter, after the sight of the pottery, was the large shallow basin from which a duct flowed down the rock dome, surrounded by a groove. This was one indication of the way in which the living rock had been used for such different purposes at different times. Inside, there was an armchair excavated out of solid rock and little shelves cut around it. The layers of sedimentary rock inside were colourful, stained with iron. Above all, the view from the overhang was breathtaking.

11 *The rock overhang from the side, with the excavated standing stone on the near horizon*

12 *The basin and groove on the roof of the overhang*

13 *The 'armchair', made with metal tools*

This section is about time layers. In an archaeological record this usually means bands, time zones in a section in a trench. Here it meant more, for the use of the shelter was in itself a cross-section through time. Given the natural outstanding position and formation of a cave-like feature, people used it for different purposes. The hunters would have sheltered in it, but so did people using it thousands of years later, for the opening had been screened with a low wall and wooden props made a shelter framework to keep out the weather. This happened possibly as late as the time when it was used by those who drank from glass bottles and tea cups, who may have used a penknife to whittle wood or to cut tobacco. They were unaware of the previous presence of the hunters or of the dead person at their feet. Had they suspected that something lay buried there, they would surely have dug it out, in which case their disappointment at finding nothing more than what looked like an old cracked flower pot may have led them to discard it.

Perhaps one observant person noticed a faint peck-marked groove running down the shelter floor; the marks were not made by the metal pick used to create the armchair. It led towards the small triangular slab embedded in the floor that had led to the discovery of the pot beneath it. This brought me to the site, which no one before had investigated archaeologically.

I visited the site after pieces of the rim of a pottery vessel found there were brought to me. The pot stood upright in a pit dug through the rock floor; sometime during this operation the Mesolithic material was disturbed. The pit became a sump for the water that blew in on the wind or trickled along the floor. It was what archaeologists call a Food Vessel (see chapter 8), decorated with impressed marks. It had lugs that had been stuck on when the clay was wet, and was full of cremated bone and charcoal. As there were no signs of burning on the shelter floor, the body must have been cremated elsewhere. Then the triangular stone was placed over the pot rim, disturbed soil stamped down over it, and there it lay for about four thousand years. In that time we do not know how often the shelter was used, but the floor remained undisturbed and any dropped fragments became part of the soil on the floor. The base of the pot had suffered from being in a sump, so it was lifted with its immediate surrounding soil and transported to Newcastle University.

It is often necessary to lift out a pot in this way, for it can then be excavated in laboratory conditions. This happened too at Blawearie (below), when an inverted enlarged Food Vessel was lifted from its pit and sent to the British Museum for excavation and conservation.

Laboratories are the best centres for analysis of the contents of such pottery. Contrast such conditions with those of some of the early diggers such as Canon Greenwell who excavated a burial at Chollerford in 1847 by candlelight in six inches of snow in a high wind, where he discussed the 'mouldering remains' on his knees while the workmen stood around!

The other artefacts are part of a later story, but the rock shelter has many important things to say about prehistory. It is a 'natural place', an outstanding feature in the landscape. It has been used for different purposes for centuries, as a shelter and as a burial place. Close by and leading up to it are two standing stones. Below it is a double-walled and ditched enclosure (**15**), possibly of the Iron Age, which it overlooks. It lies on a natural pathway over the scarp, linking it with other prehistoric sites, notably those that have rock art.

This is not the place to examine archaeological techniques in detail. For these, you may wish to refer to Kevin Greene's book (2002) on excavation. Some general observations follow.

About one third of all sites have been found by aerial survey. The information from the photographs is transferred to maps. Such things as buried ditches and walls still show from the air in certain conditions, such as times of

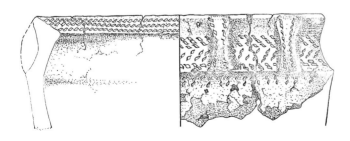

14 *The surviving part of the Food Vessel that contained cremated remains.* Mary Hurrell, NUM

drought. The sketch shows how this happens (24). Viewers of *Time Team* and other programmes will be aware of how 'geophysics' can be used to locate buried features which appear as 'anomalies'.

It is then the turn of excavation, which is designed to answer research questions. The excavations themselves can be either total or partial, depending on the site and the nature of the questions being asked. The object is to recover information not only of structures but of buried land surfaces with their pollen and carbon that tell us about what was growing there and when. There may be artefacts; there may be animal and human bones. Once the excavation has been planned, it is important to find out what a natural soil profile looks like by digging a section away from the site, but close by, to establish the type of 'natural' base of the area. All the soils above this may have been worked at various times, and may show disturbance. Once the local geology is understood, the excavator can then choose where to put his or her trenches, depending on what area is most likely to answer important questions and on how many people there are to work. Everything found is given an object number and a context number and this information is recorded on a plan and in sections. The speed of excavation depends on the type of remains, and on the experience and skill of the diggers.

All recording must be detailed and precise so that, no matter what conclusions are reached at the time of excavation, the data are available for future reconsideration, especially as more sites bring in new interpretation. Interpretation cannot depend entirely on a good recording system, for the significance of what is found is an exercise of the intelligence – being able to see the relationships between pieces of information. There can be a tendency to find what you are looking for! Richard Bradley, Professor of Archaeology at Reading University, wrote an article called 'The creative use of bias', in which he mentioned that if you put pottery enthusiasts and flint enthusiasts togeth-

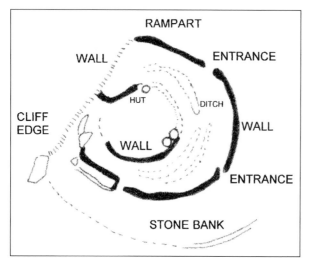

15 *Plan of the enclosure that lies downslope from the rock shelter to the scarp edge (based on an Ordnance Survey map)*

16 *The discoverer: Peter Cheffings*

er in the same field, the pottery people would find more pottery than flint, and vice versa. The most dangerous aspect of bias is if you are determined to prove a theory by manipulating the facts to fit it. A cast-iron recording system, published and accessible, should allow future archaeologists to re-interpret the evidence.

Modern excavation involves more disciplines than ever before. Archaeologists may not be scientists, and have to rely on the expertise of others to interpret their findings. They have the overall responsibility for directing the work and for interpreting it, and for calling in others when there is need for specialist knowledge. At the end, the report must be published, and as quickly as possible so that others may benefit from the information. Too often these reports are notoriously long in preparation, because the post-excavation work and writing take considerably more time than the excavation itself. Without making a complete commitment to the conclusions reached at the time of writing, the excavator should produce an interim report as soon as possible after an excavation.

Those who have not experienced the excavation may find it difficult to 'tune in' to what they see there. Trowelling and examining the soil brings us close to the nature of the whole site. Sensible organisation enables the diggers to appreciate not just their own little patch, but the whole site. The speed of excavation depends on the type of remains, and also on the experience and skill of the diggers; it is useful at the end of each day to go round the site as a group to discuss what everyone has found.

This book contains the results of many excavations that have built up for us a picture of what happened in the past at particular places in Northumberland.

3

THE GREAT REVOLUTION

BEFORE AND AFTER
THE INTRODUCTION OF FARMING

Before agriculture

If we try to pick out events that radically altered the history of mankind, one of the most powerful changes was brought about by a move from the hunter-gatherer economy to one based on agriculture. This signals the beginning of civilisation as we know it. People in the Middle Stone Age managed the landscape to fit their own needs; they hunted in small groups, gathered food, moved along seasonal routes from place to place, conserving and encouraging things that they wanted to grow in the wild. Coasts and valleys provided food and camps were established, a base from which to move through the land, presumably on well-defined and well-tested routes. We are thinking of people thousands of years ago living this kind of existence, never reaching great numbers.

They are our earliest known ancestors in this region. They existed so long ago (10,000-4000 BC) that for part of that time England and France were still connected by a land bridge; it was not until about 8,500 years ago that Britain became an island.

Some of the Mesolithic settlements along the coast may have disappeared because the sea level has not been constant since then. Generally in Britain the west coast has risen and the east has sunk – a change that also affects the estuaries of rivers. On higher ground peat has covered sites. If sites are buried, however, and no one knows where to look for them, their discovery is often by chance: farming or soil-stripping activities, for example. The chances then are that only stone tools survive, whereas much of the people's lives would have included what is absent from the record, such as wood or other plant material. These people would not keep still and give time for the accumulation of the kinds of things that later people would leave behind. The picture we have is of small, far-distributed groups moving from one campsite to another. Much of their diet may have been meat, in the form of red deer, roe deer, elk, wild oxen, wild boar and fish. Their flints would be used for hunting, skinning and scraping, but such implements could also be used for preparing vegetables.

Mesolithic tools found on the coast are dated to 7800-4000 BC (in the later Mesolithic age). A recent programme of fieldwalking and recording directed by Dr Christopher Tolan-Smith has concentrated on inland valley sites along the Tyne valley from Newburn to Warden. Previous work had established sites at Warden and Corbridge on terraces above the river valley, a good spot for people who relied upon hunting, gathering and fishing for their survival, and who may have lived for longer periods of time on the coast: they might have been able to move inland by water.

I have written about Warden Hill elsewhere (Beckensall 1998); its dominant position above a glacial terrace north of the rivers North and South Tyne close to the place where they meet has attracted people to use it for farming, ritual and defence. The Mesolithic sites, two of which were found by Joan Weyman, occupy the south-facing sunny slope above the river, known only from a scatter of flints. My first encounter with a new site was from rabbit holes beside a public footpath. Evidence for Mesolithic activity is, however, slight; the flint and quartz implements found do not amount to many. What is significant is that from all the fragments found it is clear that people used the slopes as places where they actually made their tools from raw material either found locally in gravel deposits or brought with them. On its own the finding of flint scatters is not enough, and such sites invite literally in-depth excavation that alone can glean the whole range of artefacts.

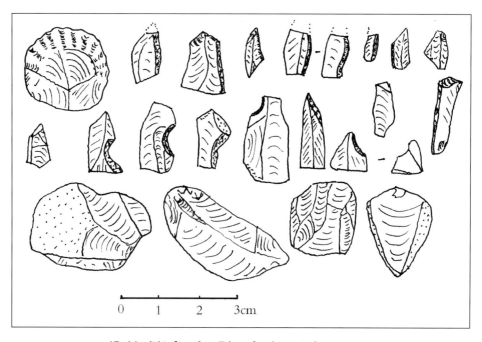

17 *Mesolithic flints from Felton, found in a single visit*

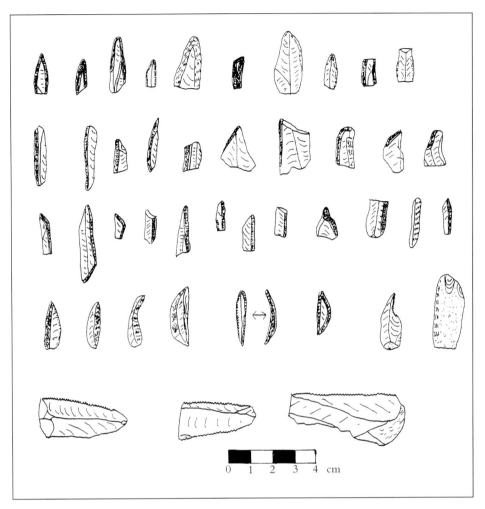

18 *Part of the Berthele collection: mainly microliths from many sites*

At Felton Park (Beckensall 1976, *Life and Death in Prehistoric Northumberland*) I had an earlier opportunity to find evidence of Mesolithic activity that came from a hunch. During one of my walks along the high north bank of the Coquet I noticed that a field had been ploughed. Having thought that such a location would have made a good campsite for hunter-gatherers I put my idea to the test. The flints were there on the surface. The flints from Warden Hill and Felton are now in the Museum of Antiquities, but my exploration has gone no further than that. Warden Hill was visited several times; Felton was ploughed only once while I lived near there. There is much follow-up work still to be done.

The number of places where Mesolithic tools have been found continues to increase, pushing the sites over a much wider area. Fieldwalking, using a grid system to record precisely where flints are found, has led to a more accurate picture of where these scatters are. For example, there was little in the Cheviots; now there are many, including flints from the Breamish Valley Archaeology Project at Turf Knowe (see below). What is happening is that the more one recognises the thin blades of this culture and the significance of the chippings, the more one discovers such things among established collections. Fritz Berthele's collection of flints on areas ploughed for new forests is rich in microliths. Should such areas become available again to investigate, there is a wealth of information waiting there.

Fritz, who came to England as a prisoner of war, stayed here and married. His work for forestry was rewarded with a BEM, presented by the late Duke of Northumberland. I first met him through our daughters, who went to the same school in Alnwick, at his home, where I was also introduced to his amazing collection of flint implements and other artefacts. I made preliminary recordings of his collection, and took much of it to the Museum of Antiquities in Newcastle to be drawn. There it came to be examined by other archaeologists. Later, Ian Hewitt (1995) was to record the locations of items in his collection, which is now in Chillingham Castle.

The illustrations in this book show the extent and variety of what he has found. It ranges from microliths through to Iron Age times, and indicates an extensive use of the landscape that was not realised before. These finds are from the surface only.

The most recent large-scale investigation of a Mesolithic site was carried out by Clive Waddington of Newcastle University on the cliff top at Howick (forthcoming), following his investigation of early sites in the Bolam area (Waddington 1998). It is possible that some of the site has fallen into the sea, for this is the general pattern of east coast erosion; what is left is a substantial area of fine sand lying on sandstones and shale, visible in section along the coast in some dramatic patterns, acidic and therefore not good for preserving any organic material, unless it is burnt, but containing a substantial number of Mesolithic tools, weapons and waste flakes. The excavator has allowed me to use his interim report to bring this very important site to the public in advance of its publication.

Excavations took place in 2000 and 2002 at NU 2585 1660. There were pits and scoops, a circular Mesolithic structure that showed up as stains of laid timbers, post holes and sockets. The main structure was circular, sunk into the ground, with timbers and postholes. Here people had lived, and the use of the building included a succession of hearths. Twenty-one radiocarbon dates showed that the site was constructed in c.7800 BC, which is considerably earlier than any other in the county, and that its use extended over two or three phases. It is one of the earliest known and preserved sites in northern Britain.

The burnt bone from the hearths included wild pig, fox, birds and either dog or wolf. Charred fragments of bone, hazelnut, acorn shell and marine shells were included in the debris, as well as flint and ochre. Over 18,000 flints

19 *Howick excavations, 2002, directed by Dr Clive Waddington*

were excavated, which makes the recovery of such things from other sites very sparse! The making of tools was obviously of great importance there, including scrapers, blades and microliths, made mostly of flint, but with occasional quartz, chert and agate.

Part of the site had slipped into the sea with the rising sea level. The importance of the site cannot be overemphasised. There is now more information about coastal settlement on a permanent or semi-permanent basis, and further analysis on radiocarbon dates may well add more information. A replica hut based on these discoveries has now been built on the Maelmin site at Milfield village.

This is one of a number of sites along the coast that show how hunter-gatherers favoured places where seasonal plants and animals were there for the taking, especially fish and shellfish; at Howick, hazelnuts were also on the menu. These coastal and other sites have been documented by John Davies (1983), and include concentrations at Holy Island, Ross Links and Newbiggin–by–the-Sea. As the coast becomes more eroded it is possible that more sites will appear. Recently at Low Hauxley, early Bronze Age burials in cists were exposed during violent storms in 1983 and 1994 (Hardie 2000). If a close eye is kept along the coastline, more prehistoric sites of different periods may come to light.

As we move from one major prehistoric period to another, in this case from Mesolithic to Neolithic (which is from *neo* = new, *lithos* = stone), the general picture seems to be that there were more people exploiting more of the landscape, and in a different way, for people began to settle down, to make the more permanent homes essential to growing crops and the herding of domestic animals. Instead of limited clearings we begin to have fields. Yet the nomadic element does not depart from their lives: there was grazing to be sought on the high grounds and slopes, animals to be hunted for food and clothing, herbs and other plants to be brought back to the settlements.

In later periods different kinds of survival of settlements, burials, cairnfields and field systems are revealed in a different way. In the uplands this is because the ground has been little disturbed that these features are visible, whereas in the lowlands they occur as cropmarks or scorchmarks seen from the air or when the ground is disturbed by ploughing, building and quarrying. There are some aspects of life that may not appear in the archaeological record. It is difficult to find evidence, for example, of fishing, hunting or food gathering. The signs may not have been read, or in some cases commercial interests have ignored them. For the past to be recognised it needs people who look carefully and know what they are looking for. What has happened recently in Northumberland to redress the balance of chance encounters is that a programme of survey has been undertaken, with considerable results. The upland areas in particular have been systematically surveyed, as well as aerial survey of the lowlands.

How and why did farming begin? The clearing of forest is the major sign that people were moving towards settled farming. Local people who came into contact with this new way of life would possibly have seen advantages in it and adapted to it themselves. We don't know whether farming was the result of people coming in from abroad with their crop and animal husbandry or whether the local people adopted the systems that they saw working to such advantage for their neighbours. The rate of this change is important; we have to think in terms of hundreds of years. Anyway, it is thought to have happened about 6,000 years ago. One way we recognise a difference between the two groups is by the form of their tools. Another is the pollen record, because the new agriculture changed the natural vegetation.

All plants have pollen grains that are individual to them; they can be recognised when the soil containing them is examined under an electron microscope. People with the skill to recognise such plants compile the results of such analysis, counting the grains. What they see in this case is that woodland plants decrease in number as trees are felled or burnt and cereal crops, weeds and grasses become more frequent.

Agriculture led to settlement at a specific place. Farming tied people down to the seasonal tasks of clearing woodland and scrub, ploughing, sowing, protecting crops, harvesting and storing. Animal husbandry involved selection for breeding, fencing, protection from wild animals, and the movement of stock beyond the farm for seasonal pasture. This different way of life demanded developments in house design, in tools, and in the way the land was divided

20 *Lynchets and rig and furrow at the junction of the Elsdon and College Burns*

up and used. It provided a base for population to increase, which in turn put more pressure on the exploitation of the land in times of difficulty, more colonisation, more rivalry and more struggle for resources. Those people who have looked at the prehistoric past as some sort of peaceful era ruled over by a benign Earth Mother will have to think again, for the roots of conflict are deep. (Read William Golding's *The Inheritors* for a symbolic account of evil coming into the world, when simple nomads encounter a more sophisticated and amoral group.)

Settled farming and adaptability, and a realisation of the benefits of innovation meant that some communities could thrive, become rich on a surplus. People like to show their wealth; the search for exotic items that could demonstrate this to others shows itself particularly in their grave goods. These symbols of power are attractive and have drawn our attention to them, but are only a small part of the story. What really matters is that the base of wealth expanded, and that has always been the result of good land management.

Britain is not homogenous; it has very different regions where wealth-creation depends on what was already there: the kind of terrain, its fertility, the ease or otherwise with which it could be cultivated. Primitive tools were, in general, effective on light, well-drained soils such as gravels or chalk. Thick heavy clays would eventually be taken into cultivation, but those who had the lightest and richest soils had a head start.

Intelligence is a crucial factor, not only in adapting to places where people chose to live, or had to live, but in seeking ways in which to make a living and to create a surplus. Ingenuity was needed not only to come to grips with terrain, vegetation and soils, but also to build houses, stockades and monuments. When people today visit henges, stone circles and megalithic tombs or the ramparts of big hillforts, it is obvious that someone in the past has faced and solved many engineering problems.

The orientation of some monuments suggests a grasp of elementary mathematics and astronomy. We can be impressed by the quality of pottery, jewellery, flintwork and metalwork. However, we must consider the time scale for the creation of these things and for their frequency or rarity. Hillforts are far removed in time from megaliths, as are the first metal tools from those made of flint.

21 *Part of the Berthele collection of flints*

4

SETTLEMENTS
AND DEFENCES

Introduction

What are we looking for when we try to locate early settlements? A permanent settlement is generally regarded as something bigger than a temporary camp; it implies enclosure of land for fields and for housing.

We tend to think of fields as they appear today: usually rectangular areas hemmed in by stone walls, hedges and fences. Large-scale modern agriculture has demanded that these fields become bigger and bigger. Many hedges and walls have been destroyed in the process.

Prehistoric fields must have been defined areas in cleared spaces. Once woodland had been removed on a large scale or in patches, a distinction was made between fields for arable and for animals, including their pasture and hay. Clearances were made with the use of axes and fire. One way of enclosing land was to dig a ditch or parallel ditches and to make the earth and stone upcast into a wall. This could be topped with a fence or hedge, preferably using a quick-growing hawthorn or something similar. One priority was to keep animals off a crop; another was to keep out scavenging animals such as wolves; a third was to define ownership. Within the complex of fields there would be an area where people could have their homes; this too could be fenced off. Part of the process of woodland clearance was to provide for building house walls and fences. Digging ditches and accumulating wood are basic activities in making settlements. They also enabled them to have a basic defence; later, Norman motte and bailey castles used the same materials. Just as the castle sites were modified by the replacement of wood by stone, so were some of the early house sites. Defence and right of ownership were built into these structures.

It is not good practice to take a settlement out of its landscape and study only that; it needs an agricultural base. That means that we have to look for the fields, woodlands, pastures and trackways that served it. Any visible settlement will be the last of its kind on that site; there may be others underneath it. The pattern of fields may also represent a final use of the land in prehistoric times; below these fields may be earlier ones.

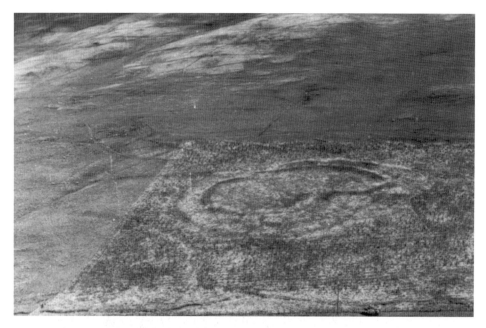

22 *An enclosure on the east bank of the Elsdon Burn. I took this photograph over 20 years ago before trees took over the site*

To attempt to separate one use of the same site from another earlier or later is a complex task. It is possible to study the subtle differences within landscape through meticulous survey. Today this has been made easier because surveying with the help of satellites (GPS) can fix a point on the earth's surface precisely; this enables one person to survey a large area, given time. Once the results are analysed, assuming that the landscape is familiar in detail from the ground as well as from the recording, a detailed plan may reveal uses of that landscape at different times. For example, wide rig and furrow running down the hillslope in a curve is usually attributed to medieval ploughing with a team of oxen. Cord rig is much earlier. Lynchets and terraces may be earlier still and continue in use throughout history.

Photography from the air or a hill at different times of the year can reveal considerable information, especially of sites that show up as cropmarks or parchmarks.

Ground radar surveys can look for 'anomalies' below the surface without disturbance, revealing many hidden features. Changes in vegetation may reveal ditches or hidden walls, pits and hut sites. Ultimately it is the excavation of a site that reveals the story of its development. Buried soils with their pollen, burnt material, pottery, artefacts or bones may point to the specific periods of occupation. It is like the layers of an onion: one skin is peeled off to reveal another, but not so symmetrically.

23 *Flodden Edge: a rectilinear enclosure seen as a crop mark.* NUM

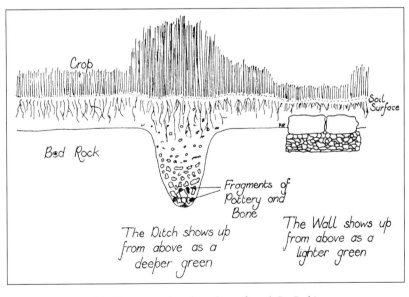

24 *How crop and parch marks are formed.* R. Parkin

25 *The Milfield Plain from Gled Law to Wooler and the Cheviots*

The earliest settlements

There are many prehistoric hill enclosures and field systems visible in Northumberland, but there are problems of tracing earlier settlements.

Earlier archaeologists tended to see only the latest episode in land use and settlement. At one time it was thought that all stone-built round houses were Iron Age or Romano-British, and that hillforts were all of the same period. The term 'Ancient British' was often used as an all-embracing term that covered hundreds of years.

Although a basic dating system based on artefacts was developed, there are more sophisticated methods of establishing period. The period from the beginning of agriculture to the Romans is a long one: about 4,000 years. That is twice as long as the distance between the coming of the Romans and us. In that prehistoric time climate has changed; an increase in rainfall, a rise or fall in temperature can make a big difference to what is to be grown. The cultivation of land can ruin its fertility, especially in areas of thin soil; this drives people away from marginal land into the more fertile lowlands, but may also cause starvation and strife.

What is known about early settlement sites? In Britain very few of them have been found. We know little about how changes associated with early farming took place from the early to late Neolithic. We know from animal bones from various sites in Britain that cattle were the main animals in the early period and that the number of pigs increased, which could have happened because pigs were feeding on increased scrub woodland that may have resulted from the decreasing quality of some soils. Archaeologists have to rely on finding domestic sites, but there are very few nationally. Stone houses like those at Skara Brae in the Orkneys, covered with windblown sand, are rare survivors. Elsewhere the record has been blurred by so much emphasis on monuments. Most of the houses known about were rectangular in plan and made of masses of wood. Through time, houses became circular in plan, and some of the best examples are over the Border at Meldon Bridge, Peeblesshire, on a defended promontory of massive posts and wall. The excavation of this links up with the work of Northumberland archaeologists, who have pioneered investigations of early settlement sites on both sides of the Border.

Parts of Northumberland show some early settlement; Neolithic long cairns (see chapter 5) imply that there was a population to use them.

An early Neolithic site at Sandyford Quarry Field (Waddington 2002)

In a field near Bolam Lake (NZ 075 817) an early Neolithic site and a Bronze Age cairn were discovered initially by John Davies as a result of field-walking. He found a surface scatter of Neolithic flints and pottery. A team of students, volunteers and members of the Northumberland Archaeological Group led by Clive Waddington excavated the site and revealed a 'small transitory settlement'. It was fortunate that the site stood alone both in time and space, for it was possible to establish that there had been a timber-framed structure that would have supported a light roof, perhaps made of hides, within a fenced enclosure.

The dwelling was established by postholes and post pipes (the latter much thinner than the former), the largest of which were set in a triangular arrangement, and the thinnest of which suggested slender timbers as uprights. A reconstruction based on the excavated plan was built at Brigantium, Rochester, looking like a substantial ridge tent surrounded by a hurdle fence. It could have been erected and dismantled quickly.

There were domestic pits around it that produced charcoal and artefacts that dated the site to the early fourth century BC. There was emmer wheat in the pit fills that is evidence of early agriculture. Charred hazelnuts suggest perhaps a late summer or early autumn use of the site on a seasonal basis; the excavator believes that the dwelling was not occupied full-time. The pottery fragments were of Grimston Ware, similar to those found at Thirlings and Yeavering (see below and chapter 8).

The site shows that mobility continued to be an important part in the life of early Neolithic farmers. It also establishes a definite presence in the south of the county.

26 *The Milfield Plain: crop marks reveal a wealth of prehistoric and later abandoned sites on either side of the A697.* NUM

27 *Prehistoric aligned pits revealed during Roger Miket's excavations at Thirlings*

The Milfield Plain (Miket 1976, Harding 1981, Waddington 1996/7)
One of the earliest signs of 'settled' activity is on the Milfield Plain. Stray finds of the earliest types of Neolithic pottery are not always placed in a firm context, so it is sites like Thirlings and Yeavering to which we have to look for significant discoveries, although recent work at Milfield has uncovered a range of early Neolithic domestic activity on the edge of this important landscape too.

The apparently flat Milfield Plain has cementstone as its base. During the Ice Ages it became a hollow into which sands, gravels and clays were poured; as the ice melted and retreated these deposits were left to form what we see today, over 10,000 years ago. Farmers used it 5,000 years later.

The River Till enters the plain at Weetwood Bridge through a narrow valley that divides the Fell sandstone outcrops. It is joined by the Wooler Water via a glaciated valley with haughs on either side that separates the Fell sandstone from the Cheviot andesite. Further north the Till is joined by the Glen, flowing through an alluvial glaciated valley between andesite hills and their extension north to the river Tweed, of which the Till is a major tributary. As the Glen flows into the plain, it does so through a raised glacial terrace that fanned out when the ice retreated.

The plain, although it appears flat, is not unvaried. Alluvium on either side of the river and its tributaries is flanked by clays and silts, sands and gravels that have produced a variation in soil quality. The plain, with its stream and valley thresholds, was of great importance in prehistory as an area overlooked by hills that were ideal for woodland, hunting and pasture, and as a generally rich area for arable farming and pasture. It was also a centre of communication, but was prone to winter and spring flooding.

To the west the andesites are covered with rich brown earth suitable for cereals, today and in the past. To the east the Fell sandstones generally have thin, acidic soils, not suitable for arable, but suitable in parts for grazing.

Settlers were aware of these differences, illustrated by the fact that modern villages are sited on attractive terraces: Wooler, Milfield, Coupland and Doddington.

To the west the andesites are covered with rich brown earth suitable for cereals, today and in the past. To the east the Fell sandstones generally have thin, acidic soils, not suitable for arable, but suitable in parts for grazing.

Pollen cores have established Neolithic activity, when woodland clearance took place in the fourth millennium. Only at Akeld Steads has there been a core sample, showing clearance for crops 4000-3000 BC. The Fell sandstones appear to have remained wooded. Obviously more samples are needed to build up a more detailed picture.

It was not until 2500-2000 BC that mass clearance took place in the Cheviot uplands, as samples from Wooler Water and Powburn suggest, the same period that saw extensive pit alignments on the Milfield Plain. The purpose of the pit alignments with their cremated bone and Grooved Ware here and at Ewart is not certain; Clive Waddington (1997) has made a valuable con-

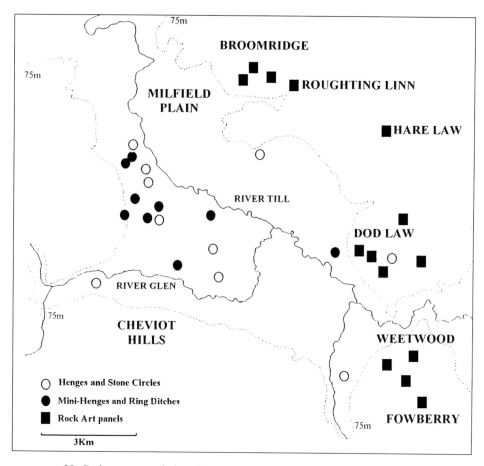

28 *Rock art areas overlooking the henges and other monuments of the Milfield Plain*

tribution to the debate on this. He is concerned that over-generalisation has obscured the fact that the use of pits is varied. Air photography has revealed most of them, as they show little or no trace on the surface. They are arranged in straight lines and are of a uniform size, made in one go. Occurring widely in Britain, they divide up the landscape. At Milfield they show up because they are dug into a gravel valley floor. Because they are so regular in their construction, alignment and depth, it implies that there was some overall planning. At Milfield, packing stones were used in the pits, suggesting that they held posts; if so they would stand in lines apart from each other with nothing between them, as far as we know. They might have been totem poles.

These pits at Milfield North are associated with henges; some, connected with ritual sites, are double lines that appear to be associated with the Milfield North henge in the late Neolithic/early Bronze Age. In one sense they are avenues; in another they are boundaries that contain at Ewart a henge and a possible mortuary enclosure. It is likely then that such an enclosed area was not for agriculture or land division, but as markers for a 'sacred' area that many could have shared.

At Milfield there is plenty of burial and ritual activity, with some signs of early Neolithic activity too. Only Thirlings and Yeavering have any domestic sites, but the Plain seems to have been settled before the henges were built. It is possible that the henges served a population that was widespread, and that they didn't all have to live on the Plain itself.

The henges are found on the gravel terraces. Elsewhere there are silts, sands and clays. It could be that later sediments have covered some of the Neolithic sites. We can speculate that the Neolithic population was widely scattered over and around the plain and in the Cheviot Hills. Traces of high settlement could have been removed by the farming activity in the Bronze Age. An article entitled *Archaeology in Northumberland 2000-2002*, p.24 'New evidence for prehistoric settlement at Milfield', having restated the important discoveries from the air of henges, a cursus and burial sites, describes how the proposed extension of a large gravel quarry there demanded an excavation. There the density and quality of remains 'surpassed everyone's expectations'. Over 140 archaeological features were recorded, mostly on a terrace. There were massive enclosures and small horseshoe-shaped enclosures, but most features were small prehistoric pits 0.3-1m in diameter. The association of enclosures and ritual sites was said to be 'exciting'.

There was a considerable amount of pottery, mostly fine Beakers in non-burial contexts. The decoration was All Over Corded Ware in the upper fills of fire pits and Coarse Ware 2m down at the bottom of a pit. Carbonised material inside showed that one had been a cooking pot. Earlier periods were represented by 15 sherds of Early Neolithic (mid-fourth century BC) and fragments of Peterborough Ware (mid-third century BC). The gravel company agreed to cover the features, where they remain undisturbed.

The Cheviot Hills

There have been important surveys and excavations in the Cheviots over the past 25 or so years that have considerably altered our ideas on how and when they were colonised.

Before proceeding further, it is necessary to distinguish between two types of settlement, recognised throughout the Cheviots: enclosed and unenclosed. The unenclosed kind is usually one or more huts made of timber arranged in a circle or of a stone base for a timber structure. They have clearance cairns where areas have been made ready for cereal cultivation or the cutting of grass for hay. Other sites, some partially enclosed and others completely, may have developed from there. Especially from the air they look like sheep stells, and were perhaps intended for stock.

Recent work (Topping 1983, 1989) has established a sequence that may change as more sites are excavated, but at the moment it goes something like this:

i) In the Cheviot Hills the earliest field systems are lynchets and terraces that run parallel to the contours. They look like those, for example, in the Mediterranean. A strip of land is created for cultivation, but it also prevents the soil from creeping downhill and retains moisture. These fields may be replaced by a system of what is now known as *cord rig*, which is narrow rig contour ploughing and looks rather like corduroy.

ii) One or more huts may be built on top of this, later than the terraces. Field clearance cairns may also represent a later system of land management.

iii) The lynchets and terraces may remain, but the land above them may be divided into walled fields. These may lie close to the houses, and may have been used for penning animals. This can happen when stock raising at that particular place is more important than growing cereals.

iv) Throughout all these minor changes, the lynchets and terraces may go on being used.

v) The last use of the land before it is enclosed in modern times is wide rig and furrow that cuts through all previous systems, curving down the hill in wide parallel swathes, looking from a distance as though the land has been combed.

These systems have survived because they have been abandoned to pasture, never to be ploughed again.

Houseledge

The excavation of the Houseledge site in the Cheviot Hills (NT 953 280) by Colin Burgess with the Northumberland Archaeological Group (mostly volunteers) in 1979 is a very good example of the search for the earliest settlements, this time in the early Bronze Age (Burgess, 1979). One way of locating such sites is the growth of bracken among the heather, for it likes richer, deeper soil that goes with settlements.

On a long ledge, sloping to a stream valley, were faint traces of huts, clearance cairns and field walls that had previously been totally overlooked. The huts lay in a line about 100m long, and the one that he excavated proved to be a circle of compact stone with an entrance. The building was about 9m in diameter, set in a ring bank made of piled up clearance stones, 1m high and 3m wide. There were no internal signs of support for a roof, but the floor was partly cobbled and partly made of compact earth, full of charcoal fragments. There was a narrow entrance and a rough threshhold slab. Finds of pottery showed that the building was in use in early Bronze Age times. Below the house floor was an earlier building, this time a 'classic ring groove house', where a curved trench is cut

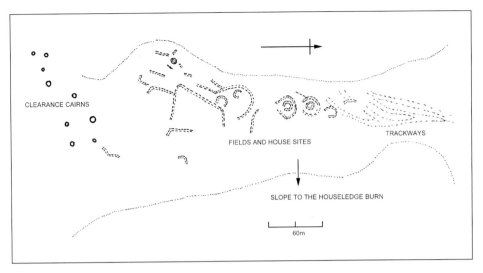

29 *The Houseledge site.* Based on C. Burgess

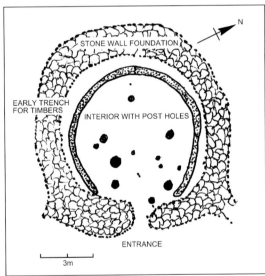

30 *The excavated ground plan of a house at Houseledge.* Based on C. Burgess

in a rough circle to take timbers that form walls and support a roof. At 8m across, it was slightly smaller than the later building. It had been deliberately filled in before the next structure was built on top. The excavator suggested that pottery finds and flints made it the earliest recorded early Bronze Age house in Britain.

This ring groove house was built over an old field terrace, part of a system that made narrow steps on a slope for small fields. These fields seem to have been replaced by large, embanked fields down to the Houseledge Burn. The people living in the house had thrown their rubbish among the fields on the slope, including bits of pottery and flints, including a broken plano-convex knife of the same period as the house. Other signs of farming lay in the clearance cairns to the west; these are small piles of stones collected when fields are being prepared for cultivation or to make it easier to cut grass for hay.

This site is not only interesting for its undoubted early Bronze Age date; earlier settlement on the gravels of the Milfield plain had been going on for at least 2,000 years previously, abandoned at about the time that the Houseledge settlement was established. It shows how people moved between upland and lowland. Colin Burgess says that it illustrates that for a while settlement moved into the uplands, but that between c.1200-1000 BC the deteriorating climate and increased wetness made the thin soils inadequate to support farmers.

The Breamish Valley

The Breamish Valley is one of the most important in the county. The river enters a well-known stretch known as the Ingram Valley before flowing north at Powburn, changing its name to the River Till at Old Bewick. It is the early stage of the river that concerns this narrative.

The most imaginative long-term study of an area in the hills has been initiated by the Northumberland National Park Authority in the last ten years, but there was other work done before this. Even before the extensive aerial and ground surveys undertaken by RCHME in the 1980s, a glance at older maps shows that the Breamish Valley area was rich in all kinds of marked settlements and field systems. They stand out easily for all to see, especially in strong low sunlight and in the winter. From the air they are amazingly clear, with the broad picture spread out to give a different dimension from what is seen from the ground, although the hilltops and slopes give as clear a picture of some areas as from aircraft. Some sites were partially excavated before modern archaeology stepped in, and this information has been incorporated into what we now know.

Two sites excavated using modern methods lie to the west of the present archaeological excavations: at Linhope and at Standrop. On the way up to these lies the dramatic survival of a prehistoric village at Greaves (or Grieves) Ash. Readers will do well to plan a walk through the Ingram Valley to include these sites, for this area is one of the richest prehistoric landscapes in the world, clearly recorded and now partially excavated. It is not only well endowed with sites to visit; it covers centuries of prehistory.

Recording such places is a job for aerial photography, followed by field survey. Even without excavation we have learnt much about the possible sequence of settlements. However, excavation is essential if we are to learn any more.

Linhope Burn (NT 957 172) (Topping 1991)

The site lies on a slope near to the famous beauty spot, Linhope Spout, a name that means a waterfall that falls into a pool. So often in this type of archaeology, on the margins of subsistence farming, artefacts are rare or non-existent, but in this case it has been possible to work out a sequence of events.

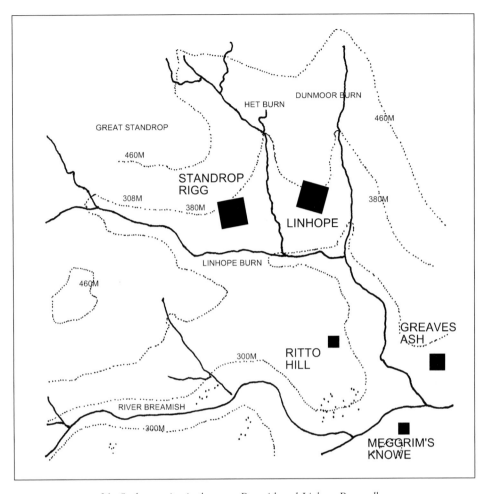

31 *Settlement sites in the upper Breamish and Linhope Burn valleys*

A notable 'first' in the Cheviots was the discovery of ard marks. These are grooves and dents in the sub-soil made by a primitive plough. Some later ones had metal tips to break up the sods; the method used was either to move the plough in one direction only or to criss-cross. Some have been found under Hadrian's Wall and its forts. At Linhope they are associated with an unenclosed Bronze Age settlement and fields. This ties in with a similar pattern to the west at Standrop Rigg.

This field system was abandoned, and later covered with cord rig that survives in a rare S-shaped swathe over 200m up, the last episode before it was finally abandoned. The settlement has two hut circles and a field system, defined by boundaries, lynchets and clearance cairns.

A most important part of a recent project has been the examination of lynchets. Peter Topping thinks that here they developed as a boundary between arable below and pasture above. Later cord rig crossed over this lynchet.

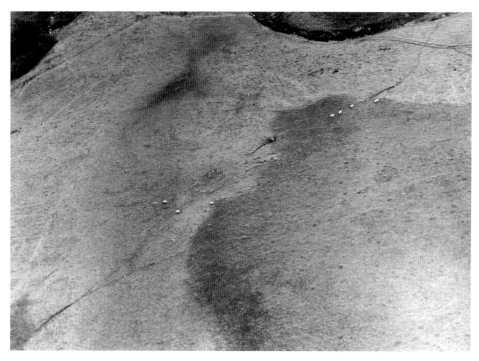

32 *Linhope, taken shortly after P. Topping's excavation. The house site is central*

Some pollen samples were taken, and showed that the early vegetation was mixed deciduous woodland with birch, oak, alder, ash, hazel and willow. There was some grassland in this partly cleared landscape. When the arable was abandoned an iron pan formed (you can see this dark grey layer in forested areas today beside forest trackways and roads); elm trees grew, alder declined, and ash disappeared. The iron pan was then covered with lines of turf, which may point to the use as land for pasture. Cord rig and arable appear, and all trees except willow decline. With the abandonment of the site birch is stable, alder declines, oak increases dramatically. By now it is mostly grassland with some deciduous woodland (25 per cent).

This is very valuable information, but there is always a warning about pollen counts. Pollen can be wind-borne and come from another place. Thus, for example, if cereal pollen is found it does not necessarily mean that cereals grew at that place.

At 350m it is very high up, but not completely exposed. There are regular and irregular field boundaries, fragments of lynchets and small clearance cairns. Today the soils are thin and poor. There are five or possibly six house sites seen as slight circular platforms or stone ring banks. Two probable huts were excavated, one larger. Spread over the field system is cord rig.

One hut, 8m diameter inside with a wall 1m thick, had two entrances and was later than the cord rig, which was seen as low ridges and furrows 40cm wide and 10cm deep. In medieval times wide rig and furrow ploughing had split them. The second site could have been a cairn or a hut circle. The third site had a lynchet earlier than cord rig, with a period of abandonment between the two. Here there were two systems of ard marks, one criss-crossing and the other in one direction.

Standrop Rigg (NT 95752 17234 and NT 95684 17315) (Jobey 1983)

Standrop Rigg has a field system that is one of the largest associated with an unenclosed settlement in Northumberland. It extends east to the Linhope site. It is among the first areas to be colonised by farmers. At 350m it is very high up but not completely exposed. There are at least 12 field plots formed by low walls and slight terraces, with some clearance cairns and five or six houses on platforms.

Two of the house sites were excavated; one was made of a ring of stones picked off the surface and some large boulders. The other, near the foot of the main slope, with signs of roof supported by vertical posts, had a more promi-nent ring bank. It had a hearth near the centre. Small stake holes point to a wattle screen division of the house space.

The excavator placed the site in the period thirteenth or fourteenth century BC. In his discussion, he pointed out that there were over 50 certain or proba-ble settlements in Northumberland of the unenclosed type with 1-12 houses in each, but with an average of less than six.

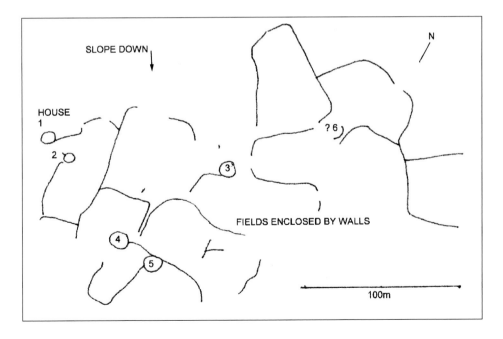

33 *Standrop Rigg settlement.* Based on G. Jobey

34 *Greaves Ash settlement towards the Breamish*

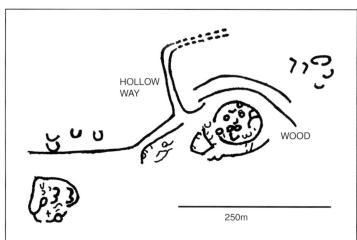

35 *A sketch plan of the Greaves Ash settlements*

The Houseledge, Linhope and Standrop Rigg sites are some of the earliest in the Cheviots. So far I have discussed the evidence of these early settlements over a wide swathe of the county. Now I turn to a more concentrated area where survey and excavation cover a variety of sites that have produced evidence from the whole of prehistory.

The Breamish Valley Archaeology Project

This project is a collaboration involving the University of Durham and the Northumberland Archaeological Group under the general guidance of the Northumberland National Park archaeologist, Paul Frodsham, planned to run for a decade.

One great feature of the project is that it has concentrated on one area; excavations have aimed at many different kinds of sites within that area, some that had appeared on surveys, and others that were unexpectedly revealed by excavation. Apparently featureless areas can conceal all kinds of interesting human intervention, opening up the possibility that there are hundreds of sites about which nothing is known.

What I write about the project is a personal statement on the results so far, based on interim reports, my involvement in some of the excavations, and on personal communication. The accuracy or otherwise of this reporting will

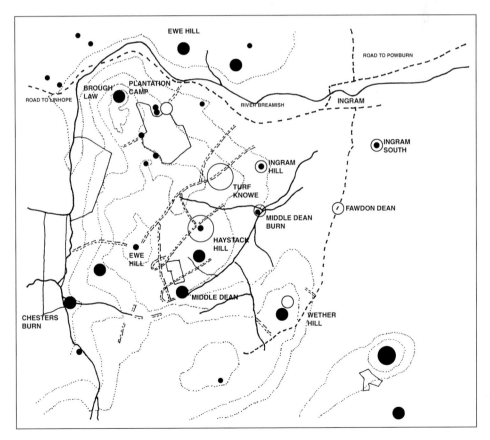

36 *The locations of sites in the text. Black filled circles are settlements and hillforts, white circles are excavated areas, and the lines are field walls. Dotted lines are access roads and tracks*

37 *Heddon Hill with its terraces, looking north from the road*

have to be set against the project's final reports, aimed at academic and popular levels of interest.

The lower Ingram Valley is accessible to walkers, well-documented and signposted, and is the ideal place to begin to understand historical changes. The hillslopes are covered with the outstanding remains of field systems of all periods. Prominent are lynchets, or terraces, where the soil is prevented from creeping further downhill by accumulated soil (lynchets) or by wall building parallel to the contours (terraces). This gives the hillsides a stepped appearance. Now some have been excavated to see how they were constructed. As motorists and hikers enter the valley from the east, there is a hill to the north, called Heddon Hill (literally, 'the high hill'), with terraces running all round it. The hill also has a different pattern of rig and furrow, like combed ridges, running downhill, cutting across the earlier lynchets. These are the two most prominent systems that we see all around us as we enter the valley. The name Ingram itself, from Old English, means the grassy slopes. In 1242 it was *Angerham*, from Old English *angr* – a settlement in the grassland. The reason why we can see the field systems so clearly is that the land ceased to be used for arable and was retained as pasture ever since. Recently some fields have again come under cultivation.

There are field walls snaking across the grassland; some are made of stone with ditches on either side, running for many kilometres. Walls can represent ownership or separation of the land into different functions such as arable and grazing. One wall close to the Turf Knowe sites (see below) focuses on a prominent large cairn, an earlier statement of territory and perhaps burial.

There are other mounds of stones that could be burial cairns or clearance heaps; it is interesting to note the absence of surface stone where it has been cleared away to make the cutting of hay or ploughing easier or to provide the material for burial cairns.

There are many enclosures, some so large that they are easy to see; others may be scoops on the hillside, circular enclosures of different sizes, large complexes of stone- and earth-dump walls that contain circular structures such as the bases of roundhouses. The most prominent are the hill ringworks, either with the stone exposed or made of a mixture of earth and stone dug out of large ditches. It is possible to see most of these even when the vegetation (especially bracken) is high, but a walk through the hills in the winter is a good time to observe, for the low sun picks out ditches and mounds in deep shadows. One very good introduction to archaeology is one of the walks planned by the Northumberland National Park from the Bulby's Wood car park, up the hill to the Brough Law hillfort and its outworks, across cleared grassland that has cairns and enclosures, across a long field wall to the Middle Dean hillfort. It is not just the immediate path area, but the whole landscape seen from the paths that is fascinating. To begin with, a map is helpful in finding sites, but after a short while you will find prehistoric features without its help.

38 *Chesters Burn; a rich area for settlements of different kinds, largely unexplored*

These sites cover hundreds of years of history. Because there are so many it may appear that the region was heavily populated, but because the time span is great, we have no clear idea whether these sites were all contemporary. Most settlement sites are comparatively small and nowhere near enough excavation has been done to enable us to make informed guesses about the number of people that the land supported at a particular time. However, extensive cultivation does point to a healthy number of people ·doing the work at various times in the valley's history.

Today the focus of settlement is Ingram village and its farms. The residents have given considerable support to the excavators, who have in turn shared their findings with them each year.

Since the fourteenth century the real decline in the settlement of the hills began, but the village remained the focus of life. The first step of the project was to consult survey work already done. Once excavation began, it was not confined to exposing a structure, but to analysing pollen and carbon samples to tell us something of the environment in the past and how it changed. Why is it that such extensive arable cultivation was abandoned for pasture? Did the soil lose its fertility? Did the climate change? A search for answers was to produce some unexpected results.

The early stages of work concentrated most of the labour force on Turf Knowe; as the name suggests this is a grass-covered hill overlooking the valley from the south. Some sites chosen for excavation had nothing visible recorded on them.

One dyke (wall) running south-west from Ingram village towards Ewe Hill and down Chesters Burn proved to be made of boulders, but some parts were

39 *Brough Law ('fortified hill'), from the steepest side. The entrance is to the left centre*

40 *Brough Law: a dominant viewpoint to Linhope. Paths lead up from Bulby's Wood*

made by excavating a ditch and piling the material into a wall. One part pre-dated some of the farming systems; it was probably Romano-British or earlier. Field systems and settlements were expected, but the Project followed where discoveries led.

There was nothing of importance marked on Turf Knowe, but a cairn was excavated with spectacular results, for it proved to be a rare 'tri-radial' type, since recognised elsewhere in the county. It was built of three walls of different-coloured boulders that meet at a point. Between the meeting place of two of these arms was a pit containing cremations in cists; one had been re-dug and a food vessel displaced in order to insert a later cremation with the decayed remains of an iron spearhead. This clearly showed that the site had been used by different peoples as a ritual/burial site from 4,000 years ago to the age of iron perhaps over 2,000 years later. Beside one of the arms of the cairn was a circular pit in which another Food Vessel had been placed on a flat stone and crushed with the weight of in-filling. There was also a horseshoe-shaped setting of boulders beside another arm of the cairn where charcoal showed that its use had extended into the AD 500s.

A vital part of archaeology is the 'sequencing' of deposits on a site; through this it is possible to work out the sequence of events. A hole dug in the ground here is not so easy to define as one would imagine, for the disturbed sub-soil has the same ingredients as the 'natural' undisturbed soil, a brash made up of shattered bits of stone. When the disturbed soil is put back into a hole it may no longer look disturbed. In trying to define the edges of the pit containing the cists, we encountered a lump of material out of which the top of a pot showed in section; it was so loose that I simply lifted the whole pot out gently before it fell out on its own (3). It turned out to be a Food Vessel of a rather plain type that had been displaced by those people who chose the same pit to bury a cremation in a cist with a spearhead, perhaps even using the same cist. It is moments like this that add to the excitement of excavation, and reward hours of patient trowelling when little else is revealed. There are moments in a dig when the whole team comes to watch something like this happening.

Down the hill away from this cairn, beside a boundary wall, excavations revealed buried soils with complex arable use, capped by an enigmatic stone structure. The cairn lay away from and above this mundane activity. When the third season of excavation turned to a new focus on another small hill, lower than the first, an important discovery was made. What appeared rather featureless, with some hints of scattered stone, was a large roughly circular cairn built on a platform. An area much larger than the cairn kerb was excavated, and in this flints from Mesolithic (Middle Stone Age) times appeared with later Neolithic and early Bronze Age flints, so rare in the Cheviots. Such a scatter meant that up to 8,000 years ago people had used the site, possibly in small hunting groups, but the cairn indicates a more settled and intensive use of the area, possibly by early agriculturalists.

The cairn was built of boulders and cobbles, probably collected from fields or from the river, surrounding two cists in the centre. These were not the only

41 *Turf Knowe tri-radial cairn: a cist which contained an iron spearhead and cremation*

42 *Turf Knowe north cairn, with central cist and another marked by a ranging pole*

burials, for scattered apparently randomly throughout the cairn were cremated bone fragments and broken pottery. At least 17 cremation burials, some in pits, were located outside the cists, with probable dates of close to 4,000 years ago. There was also in the surface rubble of the cairn a well-made and intact invert-ed Food Vessel that contained a cremation. The central cist was sunk in a pit that had two small cup marked stones and a possible saddle quern (a primitive device for grinding corn by crushing the grain with a hand-held stone) set into its edge. Another possible cup mark was found on the edge of the cist cap-stone. Cremated bone of more than one individual was found in the soil under the cover, a Food Vessel on its side, flint flakes and beads. The second cist was particularly well made from a compact, shiny stone quarried from a nearby hillside; it contained several separate cremations sealed in with a flat capstone. Part of the cairn had been ploughed into, as sharp cuts in some of the stones showed. Two complete rigs and furrows were excavated, and there was an ear-lier plough soil under the cairn kerbs. Mixed with the ploughsoil were very small pieces of Bronze Age pottery made locally.

The number of recorded early Bronze Age Food Vessels in the Cheviots shot up during these excavations, and Beaker pottery was to be added at a nearby dig on Wether Hill. Interesting though these artefacts are, a major objective of these excavations was to find more about how people farmed and lived. The finding of two such important burial cairns was unexpected, and they had to be explored thoroughly as part of the landscape. It gives the media a good story, and arouses public interest, but there are other objectives that lead

43 *The Ingram Valley east to Beanley and Powburn*

often to no artefacts or significant structures. This kind of excavation can be hard and frustrating work.

Closer to the village, at Ingram South, on a platform behind the village hall, a site revealed from the air by parchmarks was a buried pre-Roman or Romano-British enclosure, which when selectively excavated showed that barley had been stored and processed there. Carbon dating showed that this had taken place in about AD 150.

No excavation had been arranged before to investigate the fields them-selves, and this was the next task of the project, beginning with the terraces that visitors walk over when they make the ascent from the car park to the top of Brough Law. Terraces are one answer to the difficulty of ploughing on a steep slope and for the retention of moisture, and the practice is still wide-spread in the world. In the Breamish Valley the systems are fossilised, and some of the horizontal walls and small fields are crossed by later, wide, curving rig and furrow systems that follow the hillslopes down.

The contrast between the two systems makes them easy to pick out but they had not been dug or dated. With the discovery of evidence of earlier groups of people using the landscape, and the certainty that there are many visible Iron Age and Romano-British settlements, it is possible that fields may have been set out in pre-Roman times and continued to be used by later people.

The project over two seasons put very long trenches through terraces below Brough Law and close to an ancient enclosure recently cleared from forest (Plantation Camp). Beginning with two small-scale explorations, it soon became apparent that the walls of some of the terraces were of monumental proportions, with massive pyroclast boulders incorporated, equal to those used to make the tri-radial cairn on Turf Knowe. Other walls were made of smaller stuff. In all, three terraces were trenched; the walls were not built until plough soil had accumulated, so the walls were built to prevent the soil from slipping downhill. A very deep trench was dug through the fields, and the underlying geology consisting of thick deposits of water- and ice-washed sediments was revealed.

One of the most interesting results of soil sampling was the range of radiocarbon dates. The Plantation Camp terraces produced two dates: one of 1890-1590 BC, from the ploughed soil of a terrace, and the other, AD 80-260, from a stone-lined pit containing charred barley cut into a terrace. There is an Iron Age/Romano-British track that cuts across these terraces to the camp, so it is possible that the terraces were not still in use for arable then, but the early Bronze Age date suggests that the terraces were being farmed very early. One terrace there had a worn saddle quern (for grain rubbing) in its walling, and as a carbon date showed that the early soil was being turned here in the Neolithic period over 5,000 years ago, the terraces might be very old.

The nearby Brough Law hillfort and its outwork (a ditch cut outside the main walls of the fort) were built about 2,300 years ago, but the site that it is built on has a soil that was worked in Neolithic and early Bronze Age times.

44 *Terraces below Brough Law*

45 *Fawdon Dean, with Ingram village right*

It is clear from the air that many small Romano-British farmsteads survive, surrounded by field systems that do not have to be contemporary with them. A site called Little Haystacks was chosen for excavation; it had a long boundary wall beside it and field systems around. Underneath the site, excavation revealed a palisaded (fenced) enclosure of an older settlement and there were two pits of *c*.1000 BC. The boundary wall's construction was well defined, but the enclosure itself contained very few artefacts in its disturbed interior. The radiocarbon date from under the boundary wall was early medieval. It was not possible to date the field systems adjoining it – a timely reminder that although excavation is essential, it does not answer all our questions.

The 2000 season concentrated on two parchmark enclosures below Wether Hill and above Ingram South, named Fawdon Dean enclosures. These lie just off a public footpath from Ingram village to Wether Hill.

The site appeared from the air, and was confirmed by a geophysical survey, and a plan was drawn. These became the basis for excavations. One trench sectioned the later larger enclosure, in which there were parts of a substantial roundhouse with stone paving. There was much debris from occupation and destruction, including sherds of later prehistoric pottery. Several postholes marked where wooden structures had been and lots of charcoal samples were taken to provide dates. There was a coin that links the site to the Roman period. The second trench was dug across the part where the two enclosures intersected. The earlier one was at first thought to be a palisade (fence), made of massive posts set in a big ditch, but is now regarded as a substantial bank and ditch. Another stone-based roundhouse was found, cut by the later ditched enclosure, terraced into the side of the hill. With it was pottery and charcoal with paving and occupation deposits.

In Enclosure 1 the soil below the wall of the roundhouse sealed in charred willow/poplar, and this gave a carbon date of 370 BC-AD 10. The primary wall of the second roundhouse in Enclosure 2 sealed a charred alder twig that gave a date of AD 70-250. The last debris of occupation of this house was dated to AD 130-180. These dates suggest that the early enclosure was built during the late Iron Age and abandoned in the second century AD, with the later enclosure built later in the second century.

Both stone roundhouses were constructed by making two lines of stone-facing and filling them with rubble. The earlier house was 5.4m in diameter, and was built on a platform cut into the hill. The other, also 5.4m in diameter, was on slightly sloping ground. Fragments of wattle and daub show how the walls were draught-proofed. Fragments of quern stones on the site point to corn grinding, and the cord-rig on nearby hills may be the source of it. Food was stored in big jars with thick walls and flat bases. There may have been metalworking on the site.

Further work was planned for 2001, but the project was abandoned because of the outbreak of foot and mouth disease. With its resumption in 2002, work continued on the Fawdon Dean enclosures; I am grateful to Peter Carne for allowing me to use his interim report on the results. The year's work extended the area explored at the junction between the two later prehistoric/Romano-British enclosures, seen on the geophysical plot. Inside, more roundhouses were found and the house exposed in 2000 was fully excavated. Beneath this house were the slight remnants of an earlier timber house. This may have burnt down and then been replaced by the stone one on top of

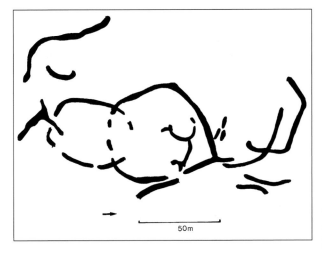

46 *Fawdon Dean: based on the 2000 geophysics results.* With permission, P. Carne

50m

it. Such houses, like so many others in Northumberland, were built on 'scooped' sites. The floor was paved, and inside was a small pit, lined with white clay for storage and backfilled with loose stones and soil. A second roundhouse, set in a stone scoop, was fragmentary, paved, with fragments of stone-walling. A third was similarly fragmentary.

What will now happen is that the considerable charcoal, soil and bone remains from the site will be examined to help build up a picture of what the environment was like. As a large amount of Iron Age and Romano-British pottery was discovered, these rare finds will add considerably to the overall picture.

Wether Hill

Another group of archaeologists with a strong voluntary membership ran a separate but related dig at Wether Hill. The hill has a large and complex series of ringworks and house sites and a cross ridge dyke. The Northumberland Archaeological Group meticulously surveyed this before choosing key areas to excavate, and began work on a piece of grassland that had only a grassed cairn visible. The cairn proved to have had its centre dug out, but a main feature was the addition of an outer kerb some distance away from the original edge. More importantly, a grassy area, which showed nothing on the surface, covered a

47 *Wether Hill area palisades, 1999, excavated by the Northumberland Archaeological Group*

48 *Wether Hill excavation, 2002, looking towards the cross-ridge dyke*

number of curved trenches for fences, marked by slots and small upright stones to take the thin timbers. These enclosures had been truncated by later ploughing, but one contained the ring-groove foundations of a wooden building. It became clearer as the area of excavation was extended that there were enclosures of different times in the Iron Age containing buildings. More dramatically, a much earlier pit was excavated that was timber-lined like a coffin to contain early Bronze Age burials.

Wether Hill hillfort

Although the fort ditches and walls enclose an area of only 1ha, the interior is packed with huts. Even without excavation, it showed many signs of change: of one system of house building and enclosure being replaced by another (McOmish 1999). The early site appeared to be enclosed by a timber palisade only 60m in diameter. When the large ditches were built the material dug out to make ditch and wall cut through parts of the palisade, which had an entrance to the east. The palisade is not the earliest sign of occupation of the hilltop, for it cuts through a ring-groove house. At the top of the hill is a burial mound with a hut cut into it; this is probably the oldest feature. There are many house sites in the form of circular enclosures that would support roofs, probably looking like the one illustrated at Butser (**56**). One task of excavation was to examine part of the interior so that a sequence is established. What

49 *Wether Hill towards Brough Law, before excavation*

came first? What kind of houses did people live in? Did they leave any signs of how they lived?

Around the hill is a large ditch with upcast on the inside and on the outside (a counterscarp). To the west is a deep, long, fairly straight ditch, especially clear from the air, that forms a major boundary of some sort. Was it built at the same time as people were living in the fort? The whole landscape around has been ploughed in different ways, with terraces, rig and furrow and cord rig visible. There were palisaded enclosures within these fields where people lived.

The deep ditch around the hillfort marks it off from lesser structures, for it would be seen from a distance and draws attention to the importance of the people living there. It could well have been the main community centre where power lay. Perhaps it was making a statement to people who had similar fortified enclosures in the area: 'Here we are. Keep out!'

There came a time when defence was not of prime importance, a time when people actually built their house foundations over the ramparts. It is the purpose of archaeology at Wether Hill to give more understanding of these changes, to find out what people were doing there for so many hundreds of years.

One very important result of excavation is the gathering of carbon dates. Over the whole site, samples taken were from birch, oak and alder, with a range of 359 BC to AD 500. Excavation in 2000 was directed at looking at

50 *Early in the 2002 excavation; uncovering previous work for continuation*

51 *Preparations for the 2002 season of excavation, showing the stone rampart*

how the rampart was constructed, what deposits filled the quarry trench, the nature of the stone-built structure, and the relationship between the palisade and the timber houses.

Excavation showed that the stone circular hut wall had been built on an area levelled out of previous occupation, with flat stones inside possibly to help support a roof. The outer rampart wall was rubble filled, revetted, with signs of a wooden breastwork on top. Outside the wall a substantial V-shaped ditch and a counterscarp were excavated.

The whole project has demonstrated how much use these sites have had throughout prehistory. Further excavations in 2002 will add to this picture, but the results will be too late for this publication. However, I can offer some photographs of the excavation in progress, and share the readers' anticipation of things to come.

From the wide coverage that has included many sites of different periods and uses, this narrative now concentrates on defensive sites.

Defensive sites

The Northumberland National Park Authority's 'Discovering our Hillfort Heritage' Project has produced a considerable addition to what was known about strongly walled and ditched enclosures. Despite the great number of visible sites, the limited number of excavations has done little to increase our knowledge of when all these forts were built, their purpose, or their relationships to each other. There has been some excavation recently, such as that described at Wether Hill above, and we have to rely on these sites as a starting point. The sites chosen for hillforts may already have had settlements on them. Their life span can be considerable: some may have begun in the Bronze Age and continued to be used during the Roman period.

Basically, a site may be enclosed by a fence or 'palisade' rather like a fort in an American Western. A stronger and more elaborate version will strengthen such a fence by mounting it into a wall made of stone and earth. A ditch is usually dug to provide upcast for the wall material, and helps to increase the size and protection of the enclosing wall. The wall itself may fall down fairly soon unless it is strengthened by a layer of stone on either side. A gateway may be a weak point in defence and need extra earthworks to give the defenders more chance to keep attackers at bay. Inside the enclosure is an area that may contain homes, sometimes permanent, sometimes temporary, and what we see today is the final episode of that kind of use. Such large areas of walled land are of use long after the people who built them died. They make particularly useful cattle and sheep pens.

Today these enclosures, within the surrounding ringworks, show clear, slight or no traces of huts. Wether Hill is a particularly fine example of the visible signs of hut foundations from different periods even before excavation. At others, such as Dod Law and Lordenshaw, later people use the ringworks as a focus for settlement that spills out beyond their original boundaries of containment.

I shall describe some hillforts in different parts of Northumberland, beginning with some in the Cheviot Hills, of which Wether Hill has provided a good introduction. Assuming Wether Hill to be a small village, Yeavering Bell appears like a county town.

Yeavering Bell

Yeavering Bell has some 130 hut circles inside it, but unless the climate was considerably warmer than today, it is hard to imagine people living there all the time. Even in summer today, at 360m OD it can be very cold. Yet its sheer size and dominance of the Glen valley, its access to rich farmland and its natural defensive position make it an ideal focus for the local people. In Anglo-Saxon times the valley below was a capital for King Edwin, who built his wooden 'palace' on part of a landscape that was in Iron Age and Roman times well-served with arable land.

The hillfort walls, built of volcanic rubble, run for 950m around the hilltop, enclosing two summits and 5.5ha of land. Traces of stone-arced walls that protrude from the east and west ends are earlier than the rampart that we see today. There have only been small excavations in the fort, so little is known

52 *Yeavering Bell to Glendale.* Cambridge University

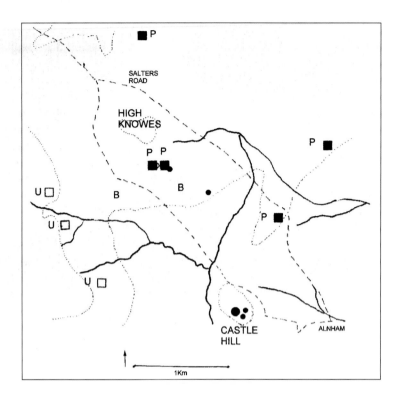

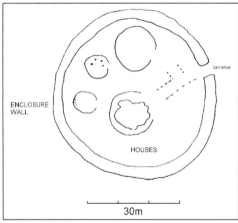

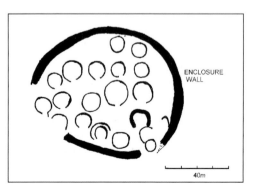

53 (Above) *Alnham: a large hillfort to the south of unenclosed settlements (U), palisaded enclosures (P), two burial areas (B) and stone-based huts (black circle)*

54 (Left) *Alnham enclosed settlements A*

55 (Left below) *Alnham enclosed settlement B*

All based on G. Jobey

56 *Dr Peter Reynold's reconstruction of an Iron Age house at Butser, near Petersfield, Hampshire*

about it. The hollows and platforms of the timber houses, with some ring groove constructions still visible, are awaiting skilled attention. One tantalising feature is a polygonal ditch around one summit, with a narrow causeway from the east. There has been much speculation about when it was built and for what purpose, but it remains undated.

Brian Hope-Taylor refers to the fort's internal huts 'being crudely excavated in the middle of the nineteenth century' and to his own excavations in 1958, when two Roman coins came from a small pit in the floor of one circular hut and three sherds of Roman Samian pottery from two other circles. In two cases two circular huts were overlaid by rectangular drystone structures associated with crude 'native' pottery. All of this is only scratching the surface.

The Northumberland National Park Authority's 'Discovering our Hillfort Heritage' project includes Humbleton Hill, near Wooler. This is a particularly exciting site to visit, not only for its structure but for its position right at the edge of the Cheviots looking across the Milfield Plain to the Fell Sandstone ridges and the North Sea. A pamphlet is available that explains the site and directs your footsteps there. It looks inward into the Cheviot Hills to Monday Cleugh, another well-situated enclosure on a cliff edge.

To show further the range of sites in this county, Alnham is one of many areas investigated by George Jobey (1966). The main visible structure is an impressive multiphase Iron Age hillfort (NZ 980 109). Nearby are three unenclosed settlements on Hazelton Rigg to the west, two groups of 'well-robbed' burial cairns, timber-built palisaded settlements, stone-built settlements and Romano-British type houses.

57 *Dod Law: hillfort in foreground, golf course and Horton beyond*

Dod Law (NU 004 317)

This prominent hillfort lies on a scarp overlooking Wooler and the Milfield Plain, at 182m OD. Basically there are two concentric ditches and walls enclosing an area of 0.3ha with stone hut circles inside and others outside extending beyond the outer defence. In the same area as the modern golf course are outcrop rocks that have some fine prehistoric art overlain by later enclosures that form an annex. It would have been reasonable from observation alone to suppose that a hillfort would be expanded by adding an outer ditch and wall, but excavation here proved the contrary: the inner ditch and wall are later.

The excavation, directed by Dr Christopher Tolan-Smith (1990) for the University of Newcastle, looked at three areas that examined the ramparts and ditches, and the annex. The project also examined the rock art in its context and recorded it accurately.

The earliest defence was built in two phases: there was a continuous fence of posts incorporated into a stone platform, with a bank of earth heaped against the palisade 1m above the old ground surface. To strengthen it, a line a boulders was laid at its inner foot. It appeared more of an enclosure for animals than a defence at this stage. This was probably in place by *c.*500 BC. To make it strong an outer rampart was built that replaced the timber fence with a stone retaining wall, its vertical face towards the fort interior. A palisade fence was built on top of this wall with a platform behind it. On the steep scarp side overlooking the Milfield Plain there were three lengths of dry stone wall with their vertical faces inward; these were used to retain rampart material, ranging in date from 385-195 BC. The excavator thought that the fort was destroyed sometime in the late first or early second century AD, well into the Roman period.

The inner rampart was much simpler, and made in one go: a double line of retaining walls about 2m apart, filled with rubble. Dod Law has huts outside the defences as well as inside. Outside there are roundhouses, a clearance cairn and a rubbish dump from which many pottery sherds were taken. The rest has been destroyed by the golf course. The house circles are still visible in the grass. Cereal grains and a fragment of quern point to corn grinding. Although the soil on the hill is thin, there is later rig and furrow for crops. Fifty-two per cent of weed pollen was from fat hen. Other pollen grains included hazel, rosehips, blackberry, raspberry, heather, bracken, rushes and crowberry.

The excavation has given a narrow insight into the hillfort, and has exposed some more pristine rock art. Sites like this produce little in the way of artefacts; people would hold on to rare valuable items, although a very nice blue melon bead, like one found in the same year at Blawearie (see below) managed to get lost. The country round about, especially the plain below and the grazing and hunting lands, would have provided a living for local people. Whether they lived in the enclosure for some or all of the time, on scattered farms, or both, is not known. A few hut circles do not point to a substantial population within the fort.

There are many more sites that repay a visit even though not much is known about them. A sequence of hillforts along the Coquet valley from Elsdon to Rothbury is of particular interest.

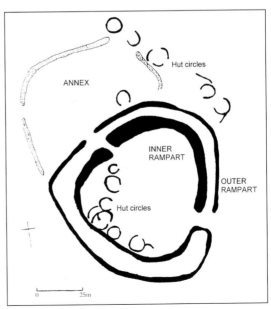

58 *The Dod Law hillfort, based on C. Tolan-Smith.* NUM

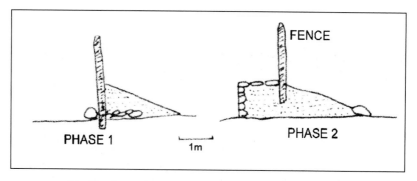

59 *The phases of rampart construction of Dod Law outer rampart*

60 *Dod Law rampart excavation*

Harehaugh

Harehaugh (NY 9695 9980) occupies a promontory that straddles two valleys, where the River Coquet is joined by the Grasslees Burn and meanders over a wide gravel plain. The defence was already provided by nature; it was left to the people to excavate deep ditches in the sandstone to form the walls that tower over the valleys. What is of additional interest in this well-sited fort is a rampart that runs across its width; is this an earlier wall later replaced by a more substantial one that enlarges the area? Is it dividing the enclosure into areas with different functions such as accommodation and stock control? An examination of the ramparts has recently been completed by Newcastle University as part of the National Park Hillfort Project to investigate the action of rabbits,

61 *Harehaugh hillfort to the Grasslees Burn valley*

which had devastated parts of the ramparts. As this was only an 'evaluation', constraints were placed by English Heritage upon the excavators; for example, ditches were left untouched. I cannot understand such a restraint, as it seems logical to have put a long trench that included ramparts and ditches through the western defences. Ditches with deep deposits of silt are crucial to understanding a site like this. An assessment in 1994 (Waddington 1998) led the excavators to believe that the site was more complicated than previously thought, with evidence of multi-phase activity. A single carbon date was thought to place the earliest phase as Neolithic.

In July 2002 a new series of 'evaluation' trenches was dug, mainly to assess what was there and how much damage had been done by rabbits; this proved to be considerable. Many of the multiple ramparts were sectioned, but even so it was difficult to establish how and when they had been constructed, as different ramparts seemed to follow different construction plans. Even the central area produced no hut circles. One is left with this large area enclosed by multiple ramparts opened up by a distinct roadway, but with almost no artefacts to tell us what was going on domestically. To the west are many deep rutted tracks, probably the result of quarrying and moving sandstone, some for the building of the fort. These quarries are many and varied, and the resulting surface disturbance can lead the unwary to think that they are the result of other activities such as the building of animal pens. However, there is, on a low ridge, a heap of stone of a long cairn that could be early Neolithic and sepulchral. Only excavation might prove it so.

62 *Harehaugh:*
rampart construction, west

What is so impressive about this and other similar sites is the scale of building, for the digging of ditches, the hauling of large stones, and the construction of concentric ramparts demanded organisation and a great deal of hard physical work.

Sites such as this on Fell Sandstone have a distinct soil profile: the natural base is a compact soil that includes bright yellow, orange and buff-coloured sands and clays. Above it the soil that forms is drained of life by acid, and it forms a grey layer of barren sand beneath a dark iron-impregnated layer under the vegetation. The contrasting colours are such that it is possible to see where the bright sub-soil has been dug out of the ditch and redeposited to make the rampart, and to allow it to be faced with sterile clay.

Lordenshaw

As we move eastward towards Rothbury through Witchy Neuk (NZ 982 994) and Tosson Burgh (NZ 024 005), we reach Lordenshaw (NZ 052 991), a fort set in an area of rock art and cairns, but also displaying a continuity of use after defence was no longer a prime consideration; here part of the ramparts has been levelled and a small village of roundhouses, possibly Romano-British, built inside a new enclosure. There is a deep stone-lined hollow way leading up to the hillfort and settlement. An early medieval deer park wall then cuts right through the rampart on the east side. Here is a landscape that shows considerable changes in use, including recent rig and furrow, stock rearing and quarrying. It is crossed by hollow ways caused by droving and the transport of stone. This is certainly one of the best and most accessible prehistoric landscapes to visit, although what is known comes not from excavation but from ground survey (Topping, 1993).

The Rothbury area is particularly rich in these hillforts; there are two more across the river to the north, and more to the east along the Coquet. Clearly the high ground overlooking such an important and rich river was a determining factor in their location.

Hillforts, as we have seen, occupy the volcanic hills and the sandstone scarps. On the latter are some fine examples, such as that on Ros Castle (Blood 1995). Not far away is the unique double hillfort at Old Bewick overlooking the Beamish/Till valley and the smaller site at Corby Crags, dominating the Harehope Burn. These can be included in a visit to the Blawearie Cairns (Hewitt 1996) (chapter 5).

63 *Lordenshaw hillfort in its wider setting*

64 *Corby Crags hillfort, above the Harehope Burn*

65 *Warden Hill: from the west*

66 *Warden hill: complex enclosures on the east*

Warden Hill

Most hillforts are in the north of the county. At the junction of the rivers North and South Tyne lies Warden Hill (NY 9041 6786), at a prominent lookout point (Beckensall 1998). As with so many other sites, its prehistory includes many periods from Mesolithic to the present. There is at the top of the hill a fort made of earth and stone walling dug from ditches, some biting into the gritty sandstone bedrock. It is typical of a small Iron Age fort, but this one has some interesting additional features that I have recorded but do not fully understand. Aerial photographs and a rough plot on the map show that there are some enclosures to the east of a rare type, probably connected with animal husbandry. There are field walls, too, and on the slopes toward the river are prominent terraces. Hollows around the main enclosure may be hut sites or shallow quarries. This site offers many research opportunities to the archaeologist.

Across the valley at Wall is another enclosure that may be of the same period. There are fewer defensive sites of the hillfort type in south Northumberland, but there are many settlements, like those at Milking Gap by Hadrian's Wall or those excavated before they were quarried for whinstone at Chollerford. At the far

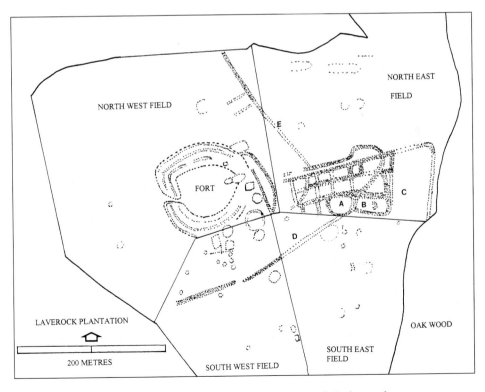

67 *Warden Hill: sketch map based on OS maps and air photographs*

south-west corner of the county is Hartley Burn Common where settlements and rock art have been recorded and recently excavated by the Kellah Burn project (NAG Vols. 15-16).

A recent survey of a hillfort at Shaftoe (Davies 1988, 1995), literally 'a shaft-shaped ridge of land', has drawn more attention to a defensive site set in an interesting and attractive landscape (NZ 052 877).

So far, the hillforts listed belong to the hills and scarps. The coast has a single rampart and ditched enclosed settlement at Howick that shares some of the simple characteristics of these forts, but this one has much shallower ramparts and a simple entrance. There are faint signs of huts inside, and in 2002 at the time of the excavation of the Mesolithic site and the early Bronze Age cists (see chapter 5), this structure was surveyed, to add to the aerial photograph already in circulation (Hardie 2000). Other fortifications of the same period are known to exist along the coast, but have been ploughed flat and only show up as crop marks.

An interesting recent survey (*Archaeology in Northumberland 1999-2000*) has shown how crop mark sites can be investigated and recorded without excavation. At Cushat Law on the Howick estate aerial photographs were transcribed on to maps as a plan of a rectangular enclosure of the Iron Age/Romano-British type with an entrance and circular huts inside. A geophysical survey, followed by two excavation trenches, confirmed some of the aerial details. This kind of survey, mainly 'non-intrusive', proved useful to the owner who was considering a shelterbelt of trees, which can be planted away from the archaeological remains.

This section now returns to a blanket coverage of an area in which there are the archaeological remains of many periods and types, including settlements and defences.

Beanley Moor, Titlington and Hunterheugh
(Tyne and Wear Archaeology Unit 1994)

I have covered the Breamish Valley in some detail because excavation and survey there are so significant and informative. There are other areas that also have very interesting prehistoric landscapes, such as Old Bewick, but I have chosen Beanley, Titlington and Hunterheugh for a little more consideration. Recently I have spent much time on the fine detail there, to the extent of making new discoveries by observation in the field. For example, although previous surveys have little or nothing about rock art, my own interest has led me to find some important marked rocks.

It is fortunate that such a large area of sandstone moorland is now part of a stewardship scheme that gives public access to many sites within it. To define it geographically: Eglingham village lies to the north in arable and pasture that ends with the outcrop of Fell Sandstone south of it and overlooks the course of the Eglingham Burn. The dipslope overlooks this valley to the east and

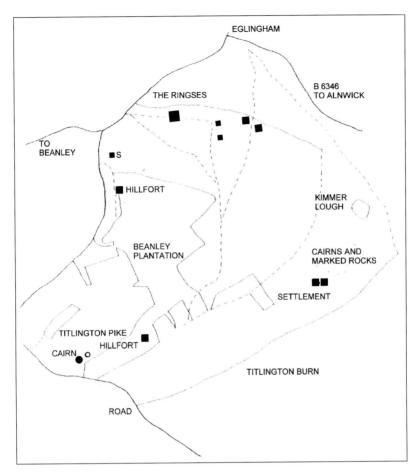

68 *Beanley and Hunterheugh Moors; principal settlements, hillforts (black squares),
the Titlington cairn (black circle) and public and 'permissive' paths*

Kimmer Lough is prominent. The west edge is defined by the road from
Eglingham to Titlington below the scarp. To the south is the Titlington Burn,
with Titlington Pike and Hunterheugh Crags rising above it. The solid geology to the west is largely cementstone, overlain with boulder clay, sand and
gravel. The flat gravel areas are now being quarried extensively, centred on
Powburn. Fertile soil extends into the Vale of Whittingham, and between
Hunterheugh and Jenny's Lantern.

There is abundant evidence on the moors of intensive quarrying for sandstone, particularly millstones. Conifers have been planted. Attempts have
been made to control the growth of bracken to allow more grassland to
develop. There is peat and there are many boggy parts off the public and
'permissive' paths. These acid soils and damp areas do not make it wholly
attractive, though it has long been favoured by ramblers. This landscape has

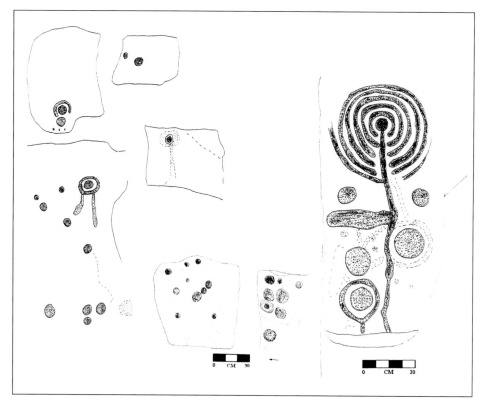

69 *Newly-discovered rock art on Beanley and Hunterheugh Moors (first publication)*

changed over thousands of years because of prehistoric activity and slight climatic changes.

The earliest signs of human activity are the cup- and ring-marked stones. Two early discoveries of decorated slabs have been on show for years in Alnwick Castle Museum – very attractive in any age. Their context, however, is vague. The more elaborate was found by workmen in 1864 about 100 yards from the Ringses hillfort (NU 0986 1861); the illustration shows a splendidly integrated design. The second came from a field opposite Woodman's Cottage (NU 08895 17546), part of a 3ft 6in x 2ft 6in x 6in slab with concentric penannulars, and is also at Alnwick. These slabs may have been cist covers. The only other rock art reported was on an outcrop mound west of The Ringses, a hill marked by a standing stone. The 'art' is not easy to see; it is only eroded cups and the odd ring.

In 2001–2 I began to look for more, and discovered one of the finest slabs in Britain, illustrated here (**71**); its location has to be kept secret until its site is excavated.

Other small, embedded boulders appear intermittently across the north of the moor. South of this northern terrace, before the rock art sites at

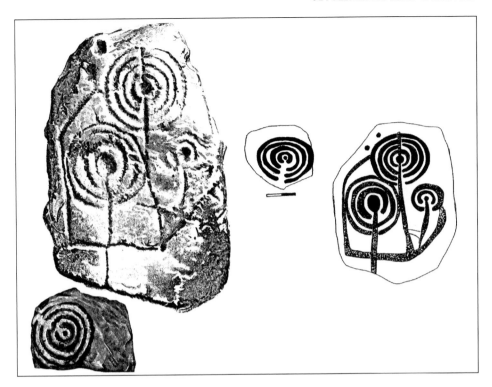

70 *Two important panels of rock art, drawn in the nineteenth century (left) and by the author (right)*

71 *Parts of an outstanding rock art panel, recently discovered*

Hunterheugh are reached, there are standing stones and boulders, some with single cup marks, one notably among a group of cairns just east of the sandstone edge towards the valley. It is likely that more will be found.

I have published most of the Hunterheugh rock art; a recent addition is just north of the footpath from Titlington to Eglingham after it crosses the gas pipeline, a scalp of rock with many cups, north of which is an unusual small enclosure of unknown function or date. Those recorded already are cups and rings on outcrop and among cairns along the south-east edge of the Hunterheugh Crags (Beckensall 2001b).

The link between rock art and monuments and cairns is well-established in Britain, giving a late Neolithic/early Bronze Age date for its use over a thousand years. There are some recently-recorded cairns on Beanley moor, but the most prominent and the largest stand on the top of Titlington Pike. Nearby is a large standing stone, one of many (some unrecorded) that can either stand naturally or have been artificially erected.

Enclosures form some of the most interesting features of these moors. None has been excavated, so we can only guess at their dates by reference to others that we know more about. They probably range from c.800 BC to AD 400. They were made by digging a ditch or concentric ditches, piling up the upcast between stone courses to make a wall. The largest stand out in the crowd: The Ringses, Beanley Plantation and Titlington Mount. Others are farmsteads that needed protection or definition, on a smaller scale.

The Ringses (NU 0999 1860), as its name suggests, is made up of ditches and walls arranged in rings, which do not enclose a very large area; the interior has only two circular hut sites and a shaft (probably a modern intrusion). There are two opposed entrances to the east and west. The ramparts are dramatically large; from afar the site looks like a giant doughnut, but parts have been nibbled away by quarrying. Outside the fort there is faint cord rig in parts, with low field walls. There are traces of hut sites and small cairns.

Plantation Hillfort (NU 0929 1781) is in a wood, high on a crag, and if there were no trees it would command extensive views – a good reason for supposing that this was the case when it was built. A path leads to it from the road through the wood; it is difficult to appreciate the plan and scale because of the trees, but there is a grassy area inside with signs of hut circles.

Titlington Mount Hillfort (NU 096 161) is not at the highest part of the ridge, for that is occupied by large burial mounds, but further east down the slope. My photograph shows it just after the tree cover had been removed (**72**).

Hunterheugh (NU 116 166) has two enclosures on a spur below the crags, so their position is not the highest point in the landscape. Although they are well walled, using in parts natural outcrop, and ditched, they appear to be enclosures rather than hillfort defences. There is a hollow way running past on the north side through the crags. Outside the second wall of the eastern enclosure is a clear hut circle. The western enclosure appears D-shaped, with signs of walling inside and a big hut in one corner where the enclosure wall ends at outcrop. There is a flat space between the two enclosures. The site was used as a millstone quarry, and one is still attached to the parent rock. Across the valley to the south at Jenny's Lantern are similar enclosures and a panel of rock art.

Beanley West Moor Settlement (NU 09143 18267) is well sited on the same ridge as the Plantation hillfort, with views to The Ringses and over the

72 *A hillfort at Titlington exposed recently by forest clearance*

73 *Hunterheugh: right of the track are Iron Age enclosures. To the left is the crag with rock art and cairns. Ahead is the Titlington Burn*

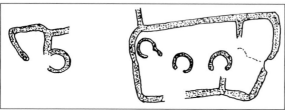

74a *Beanley from the north, with a central small rectilinear settlement*

74b *Plans of two late enclosures on north-east Beanley Moor*

Breamish valley. Ditches and low walls enclose an interior that has signs of huts and other area divisions. It is 60m east-west and 55m north-south. The entrance seems to be at the south-east corner, 4m wide.

West Corbie Crags enclosed settlement (NU 1081 1841), another place named after the crow family, is different from those so far described. No excavation has been done. It is quite well preserved, built on the same terrace as the Ringses as a small rectangular enclosure of a single 1m-wide rampart made of earth and stone rising above 1m, enclosed by a 5m-wide ditch. It has an eastern entrance flanked with stones.

Inside are three hut circles, c.5m diameter, with 1m-wide walls, roughly in line facing the entrance with their doorways. There appears to be a stockyard space between them and the entrance, with two faint sunken circles in one corner. As the ground around has no stone scatter, we may assume that the whole area was cleared. It is a very good example of its kind.

As we move further eastward, the number of enclosures increases at the end of the high ground. Some of these sites can be reached from Eglingham village, from which a footpath runs to them and beyond, southwards.

There is a cluster of huts and enclosures at NU 1081 1841 that are particularly clear in plan from the air, though vegetation can obscure them at ground level. One enclosure has 3m-wide walls enclosing a rectangle 52 x 32m, the enclosed space divided into three. Three hut circles have a yard in front of them, again a typical Romano-British arrangement. There is a detached hut circle and a sub-rectangular 34 x 33m enclosure on a slope with an entrance and one definite hut circle, possibly others. Nearby, there are several unenclosed roundhouses and stone walls of a disturbed field system. Other sites may have been ploughed out.

The crag that forms a line to the south of these sites, quarried in many parts, has a curving enclosure built up to it (NU 10602 18333). It is 70m long and 50m deep, built of coarse stone. It is possible that this could have had a continuous use as a sheepfold.

It is clear that this moorland has a very interesting prehistoric presence from Neolithic times to Romano-British, and that it would be an ideal laboratory for a study in depth (literally) through excavation.

There has been some excavation in the area, notably of two burnt mounds at Titlington (Topping, 1998) (NU 1032 1645). These are piles of burnt sandstone that have been heated and dropped into troughs of water for cooking purposes or, as it has been suggested in other parts of Britain, for saunas. Environmental samples here and from other parts of the moor have established an interesting picture of what the vegetation might have been. One mound lay on alder and hazel scrub, representing a late Neolithic/early Bronze Age period of scrub, woodland and some grass (2130-1770 BC). Then cereals appeared in the pollen record, when the scrub and heather moorland gave way to more open and disturbed ground (1670-1410 BC), after which grassy heath and moorland stabilised up to 1380 BC.

75 *A model Romano-British farm made by W. Bulmer, in the Museum of Antiquities, Newcastle*

Some of the enclosures of the Iron Age or Romano-British type that have appeared in this brief account seem to show continuity from one period to another. The major visible monument to the Roman invasion is Hadrian's Wall, which in many ways declared that Empire stopped there. What difference it made to the life of northern people, whose livelihood was based on agriculture and pastoralism can only be guessed. In the south evidence of Roman culture, such as towns and villas, gives a different picture from life in Northumberland. No doubt there was new money to be made from such a large garrison of paid soldiers on the Wall. The products of the land were always essential for feeding them. The Wall cut a great swathe across the south of the county, with its ditch, wall, vallum and roads forming a military zone. To make way for it, native settlements and fields were destroyed. Ard marks of early ploughing sealed beneath the Wall indicate arable farming, though it is not known how general this was. Had there been trees in the zone, these would have been felled for the timber needed for such things as scaffolding for wall building. Before the Wall was built the earliest Roman presence has been dated to c.AD 71, with the earliest fort established at Vindolanda. As Hadrian loved wild and mountainous country and hunting, he would have enjoyed his visit when he reportedly came to survey the line of his new frontier.

At South Shields the excavation of Arbeia uncovered a roundhouse of third century BC under the fort. Sites at Wallsend and Denton cover narrow rig and furrow systems of ploughing. Coria (Corbridge) is thought to be built over a native site. The Milking Gap native farm site excavation showed that the site, caught between the wall and the vallum, was abandoned in the 120s. At Black Carts, west of Walwick, soil sampling shows that a small piece of land that the Romans used was heathland, wet grassland and a few trees. Here the excavation of the south vallum showed that the linear mound covered ard marks which were in turn covered with hoof prints from either horses or cattle; it appears to be requisitioned arable land.

These glimpses of what lies beneath the Wall confirm that Romans did not enter an empty land, but one from which people were earning their living. Further excavation of Roman sites will help us to look further back in time, as well as contributing to our understanding of the Roman period.

5

BURIAL OF THE DEAD

Prehistoric burial mounds are among the most numerous, visible and exploited monuments in Britain. Known as 'tumuli', barrows and cairns, the latter term being used only for mounds made of stone, they have been the objects of greedy digging, with the prospects of 'treasure' within them. They have been a source of legend, which in some cases has protected them with stories of guardian spirits who will wreak vengeance on those who disturb the dead. Not only are thousands of mounds known from various sources; many have been destroyed and ploughed out in ancient and recent times. They have been seen as immediate sources of tangible history, for their contents may include pottery, implements and ornaments. Occasionally, there has been the added excitement of the discovery of gold in them.

An excavation might attract the owner's or scholar's friends, who wanted to be present when the mound was opened up and the burials reached. We have pictures of ladies in long dresses, with parasols, watching as the workmen open up the trenches with pick and shovel. We have some reports on what the results of these excavations were, some more detailed than others. Pottery and other artefacts had a fair chance of surviving this intrusion; bones and other finds were often ignored or destroyed. Fortunately the early barrow diggers included some people who developed a system of recording what they discovered, enabling us to understand more about the burial structures and how they evolved.

Burial mounds

The study of burial mounds has changed considerably since these pioneering days, as so much else has changed in archaeology, even in the last 30 years. It is no longer the contents of a mound that are of sole importance; the recording and understanding of the mound in a larger landscape context is crucial. Some have undertaken the scientific study of buried soils, inhumations, cremations and carbon within these mounds, which gives us considerably more information about the buried people and their environment. As more is revealed about how and why these mounds were built, the results point to a much greater complexity than was once thought. Some of our own examples in Northumberland will testify to this complexity.

First, however, a little background information. When people die, unless they are buried their bones will disappear without trace. In the past this must have happened to the vast majority of people. Burial implies that there is more to the disposal of the dead than this. There is a ritual that involves a choice of place to bury the dead, a way of burying the body, and the erection of a monument above it that places it firmly in a setting or context within the landscape. Burial may begin with a single body, but the site can be modified and enlarged.

Neolithic burials

Burial practices change in time; the earliest type being a long barrow during the Neolithic (New Stone Age) over 5,000 years ago. As with later burials, some of these long mounds took their material from trenches, in this case along the axis, on either side of the mound. Some mounds in southern Britain covered a wooden structure that served as a mortuary enclosure in which bodies were left to rot or be devoured by animals and birds. Some had no bones in them. Others were built over the mortuary house where bones were gathered in heaps and deposited not as intact skeletons. There are not many 'grave goods' from these early mounds. In areas where there is stone, chambers, entrances and passages might be made before they were covered over. The long mounds were sited in such a way that they could be seen for miles: that is where the ancestors lay; that was the claim that a family or tribe might make to ownership of the land. Round barrows were also constructed in that period, the most dramatic being the chambered tombs of Ireland at places like the Boyne valley and Loughcrew, with the same kind of passages and chambers inside. These were decorated with spirals, concentric circles and other motifs, know as 'passage grave art'. Scotland has splendid examples, in Orkney, for example, and Clava.

The long mounds and passage graves are not the main forms of burial mound in Northumberland, which is notable for its absence of such monuments. Sites at Bellshiel, Dour Hill, Harehaugh and Warden Hill are rare and mostly unexplored.

The Bellshiel mound is 112.78m (360ft) long with parallel sides sloping to 18.29m (60ft) wide at its east end, but generally 10.67-12.19m (35-40ft) wide. Its maximum height is 1.22m (4ft). It was only partially excavated in 1935; the kerbs were flat overlapping stone like tiles, but apart from some signs of burials at the east end, there was little found. So frustrating was the process that the excavator called the mound 'a monster of degeneracy'.

There is a recently-noted long cairn to the west of the Harehaugh hillfort, built on a long natural ridge, following its line. Another has been noted in the Cheviots (Gates 1982; The Dod, NT 9870 2065).

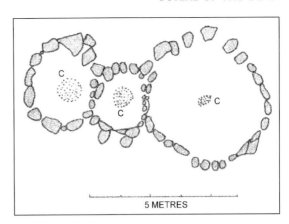

76 *Millfield Hill conjoined cairns,*
excavated in advance of forestry.
Based on G. Jobey

5 METRES

There is a possible site at Lilburn, where a unique burial of two layers of cremations in a pit that also contained two stones with horned spiral, concentric rings and curved grooves, may originally have been covered with a long mound (Beckensall 2001b). Pits and henges on the Milfield Plain seem to be more characteristic of this period.

Bronze Age barrows

All over Britain round barrows that originate in the late Neolithic/early Bronze Age about four thousand years ago are much more common – there are thousands of them. Bearing in mind that many excavated mounds have no sign of burials in them, we rely for most of our information on those that have been reasonably documented in the past or those using modern archaeological methods. There are about 700 in north-east England and about 300 in Cumbria, with inhumations, cremations, cists, 'empty' cists, grave goods and mounds over some of them.

Nationwide, these round barrows are less communal than the long mounds and passage graves, with more emphasis on the individual burial as single complete skeletons rather than a jumble of different people. Other burials focus on the original mound but extend from it. What is happening here is that the ancestors are fixed in time and place to a monument that can accommodate more as the need arises. Whereas it is possible that early Neolithic burial mounds were in clearings, on paths and in seasonal pasture because the people lived a more mobile life, the late Neolithic/Early Bronze Age fixed people more to settlements, although mobility continued for the herdsmen and hunters. Many mounds became clustered around monuments such as henges and standing stone circles, the major meeting places and ritual centres. It is possible that individual settlements had their own groups of monuments, each visible from the other.

It is mainly pottery types that give us a chronology for these burials, confirmed sometimes by carbon-dated material. In particular the distinctive Beaker pottery, common all over Britain, but varied in form and decoration,

77 *A cist at Hepburn Moor,*
drawn by Birtley Aris

and the Food Vessel (both names having been given many years ago) are characteristic of those times. These two vessels occur far more in the north-east than they do in Cumbria.

A common way of burying the dead in this period was to dig a pit, place slabs of stone inside it to form a box (a 'cist'), then pack the outside with stone and earth from the upcast. The body or cremation was laid inside the cist, sometimes with added 'grave goods' such as pottery, flint implements or ornaments, then sealed with a stone slab. Usually the slab was at ground level, the cist then being 'flat'. A mound might be constructed over the cist, in Northumberland made of the cobbles picked up from the area. Even when a mound has been removed and the area ploughed, the cist may remain intact. When a field is deeply ploughed the blade sometimes hits a cist slab and the removal of the lid reveals the contents of the cist.

Most Bronze Age burials are found in the north of the county, particularly between the Tweed and the Coquet. Many are on high ground and ridges, but some are in the North Tyne, Tyne, Wansbeck and Blyth valleys. Not so many have been found in the Cheviots or on the east coast. The picture is, of course, not necessarily the true one; it depends on how many have been destroyed by agriculture or industry, or how interested people have been in recording barrows in a particular area. Some show up only as cropmarks; the preservation of many may be the result of their being in pasture or moorland, escaping ploughing. The areas around Alnwick and Wooler are particularly well investigated, as people like Canon Greenwell and George Tate have been particularly active here. The quality of recording is an important factor.

We are looking at a period of *c.*2000–1200 BC for Early Bronze Age traditions. A thousand burials do not amount to much, hardly including all the people who lived and died in the area. We cannot estimate the size of the population from such a small number.

Very few mounds have been carbon-dated; we have to rely on pottery types: Beakers, Food Vessels, Enlarged Food Vessels, Encrusted Urns and Collared Urns. Of these the Beakers are perhaps best known generally, and have given the name to 'The Beaker People'. Beakers are diverse in size, shape and decoration; they appear both in settlements and burials, so they are not specifically drinking vessels provided for the dead in the next world (a popular early explanation). We look at artefacts associated with them, such as flint arrowheads, knives and scrapers and more exotic items such as copper daggers or a gold basket-shaped ornament from a burial at Kirkhaugh. Food Vessels are mainly confined to burials, some with flint implements, sometimes accompanied by jet necklaces. Metal objects are rarer. We must remember that 'exotic' grave goods are very rare, by definition, and we must not generalise from them.

We shall see that the other later vessels in our list are often inserted into existing mounds in the middle and late Bronze Age. In the Iron Age burial in mounds became very rare indeed; a change took place in the way people disposed of the dead.

There has been great interest among archaeologists recently in the use of 'substances' that may have been used by shamans to alter their states of consciousness. For example, in Wiltshire a burial contained exotic items thought by some to be part of 'a kit belonging to a ritual specialist'. One consideration that prompted this was that although beads are the most common objects found in rich burials in the south of England, they were not complete necklaces. Amber and jet have special properties. So-called 'incense cups' may have been used for burning substances or containing poppy seeds and hemp. Ann Woodward (2000) concludes a chapter on 'Barrows and exotic substances' with this:

> Thus the concentration of burials of ritual equipment in Wiltshire may represent the final deposition of the most precious possession of the last practising shamans of this particular cult. The already outmoded habit of ritual burning and inhaling of exotic substances may have at last given way to the alternative delights of alcohol just as, at the same time, the traditional mobile way of life gradually became supplanted by the ordered habitation of permanent farmsteads and fields. Life would never be the same again.

I leave readers to consider the evidence for this, but I will pick up the important point that she makes about mobility, for we must look at whole landscapes where barrows occur, try to see the world in the way that people who built them saw it, and seek a logic to account for why the barrows are where they are.

I have examined in detail landscapes where prehistoric rock art is found; what I have discovered applies to landscapes that have barrows. Rock art is placed at important viewpoints on high places overlooking valleys. In some cases, as at the entrances to the Milfield Plain, it directs paths to the thresholds of the plain where rivers and streams break through the sandstone scarps. Hunting, herding and gathering naturally growing foods are crucial to the survival of early people. With the advent of farming such activities continue, perhaps from a more permanent base of a settlement and its fields.

With rock art there is a change of emphasis in its use in the late Neolithic and early Bronze Age. In the open air its place commands wide views. It is sometimes pecked onto standing stones and stone circles. When it is incorporated into the material of mounds it is taken out of the open air and hidden, with the exception of the odd cup marked kerbstone of a cairn. In a very small minority of excavated mounds, rock art becomes part of the burial ritual.

Plotting barrows accurately in the landscape and showing their relationship to other prehistoric finds and sites is important to an understanding of why they are there. To move outside our area for a moment, the North Yorkshire Moors have a number of important barrows with coffins and rich grave goods; arranged along watersheds, they dominate the important ridges and declare their symbolic control of the landscape. In Britain as a whole valley locations are more common than was once thought, especially at springs and streams.

78 *Landscape with three large aligned cairns east of Ros Castle (August, 2002)*

When we look at some important Northumberland burials, we must ask ourselves similar questions about their locations. What can be seen from them, and how far away can they be seen? Are they built on sites that may already have been of significance to the builders?

It is impossible here to look at the whole range of burials in the county, so I shall take a few that represent different aspects of location, construction, grave goods, modification of structure and use over a period of time. In that way we shall see the complexity of these monuments. We have seen early Bronze Age burials at Turf Knowe (above). Barrows are only one means of burial: we see others in rock shelters, within areas enclosed by standing stones, in a wooden coffin, and in cairns that have been used for burial for a considerable length of time.

The Blawearie cairns (Hewitt and Beckensall 1996)

The excavation of the Blawearie cairns between 1984-8 was an exciting experience for many people. Arranged as a training excavation for Northumberland High School pupils, controlled and inspected by English Heritage and the Northumberland County Archaeologist, the results show just how much information can be gleaned from a site that has been the subject of much haphazard attention in the past.

The Blawearie cairns are clustered astride a public bridleway on Old Bewick Moor, named after the house nearby that was built in the mid-nine-

79 *Blawearie excavation complete in 1988*

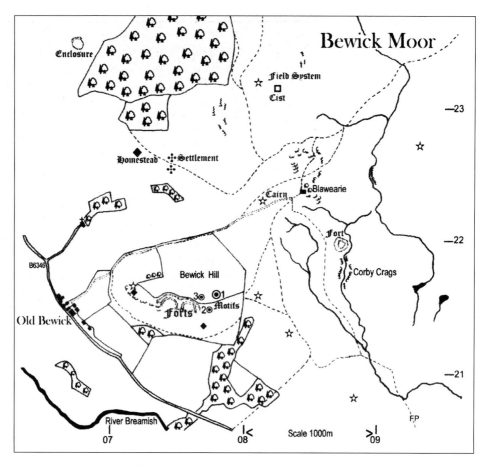

80 *The Old Bewick area: the Blawearie cairn is highlighted.* Paul Brown

teenth century, an area quarried for sandstone and used by the army for training in the Second World War. The largest is the most prominent, standing on
a natural glacial mound that it shares with two smaller circular structures. The
others, unexcavated in recent times (though at least one has had its centre dug
out), are small kerbed cairns, some conjoined, in a cluster. They now lie in
fairly marshy ground, which suggests some change in drainage since they
were built. The cairnfield is not on the highest part of the moor, but it is at
a prominent viewpoint set in a semicircle of hills, looking towards the edge
of a high scarp to the south-west and the Breamish/Till valley to the west and
north-west. It is not the only cairnfield in the area: it is overlooked on the
north-east by a cluster of burial cairns, one with an open cist, on Hepburn
Moor (a name that means 'high burial mounds'). Another trail of cairns leads
south via some spectacular rock art to a highly placed cairn on Tick Law. To
the east and north-east is another extensive cairnfield, with a particularly large
open cist and some rock art, on the slope down to the Harehope Burn.

1 *Morwick: a cliff decorated with spirals*

2 *The College Valley from the south, with Great Hetha on the left beyond the wooded hill*

3 *Duddo: part of a small stone circle*

4 *Shaftoe Crags*

5 *Across the Milfield Plain from Gled Law to the Cheviot hills*

6 *Humbleton Hill to Monday Cleugh and Yeavering Bell*

7 *Hartside*

8 *The College Valley: Great Hetha hillfort is on the right*

9 *Over Brough Law towards Linhope along the Breamish Valley*

10 *Ewe Hill enclosure above the north bank of the River Breamish*

11 *Castle Hill, Alnham*

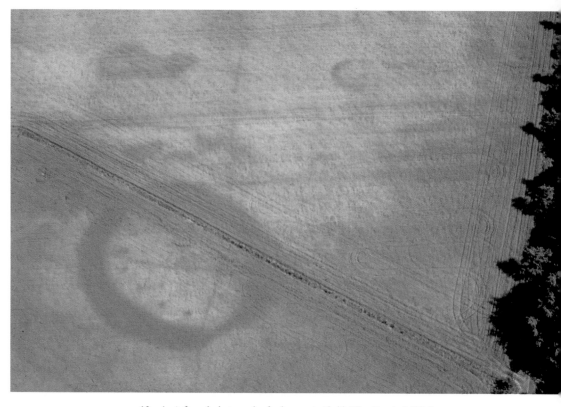

12 *An infra-red photograph of a henge at Akeld West Steads.* NUM

13 *Howick: the Mesolithic and early Bronze Age sites lie at the cliff edge in the top corner of the nearest harvested field*

14 *Wether Hill excavation in 2002. The cross-ridge dyke runs across the bottom left corner*

15 *Lordenshaw: a cairn that lies on a cup-marked outcrop, with a standing stone*

16 *Maelmin: a reconstruction of the north Milfield henge by Clive Waddington*

17 *Field systems along the Breamish Valley above Brough Law westward*

18 *Ingram Valley: from Brough Law to Beanley Moor on the horizon. Rig and furrow systems cross older lynchets*

19 *Chatton Park Hill: North Plantation divides the area roughly from top to bottom. It points towards a small hillfort on the scarp edge. To the right of the plantation is a line of crags that includes Ketley Crag*

20 *The Chatton Sandyford early Bronze Age cairn*

21 *Chatton Park Hill; decorated outcrop rock with a view to the Cheviot Hills*

22 *Ketley Crag rock shelter, with its dramatically decorated surface*

23 *Beanley Ringses hillfort*

24 *Lordenshaw hillfort*

25 *Titlington standing stone, leading up to a large cairn and down to a hillfort*

26 *Goatscrag rock overhang*

27 *The reinstated Blawearie cairns site*

28 *The Blawearie cairns excavation in 1987*

29 *Excavation at Whitton Hill east site*

30 *The central pit at Blawearie cairn*

31 *Blawearie excavation: the last deposit was this Food Vessel Urn with two cremations*

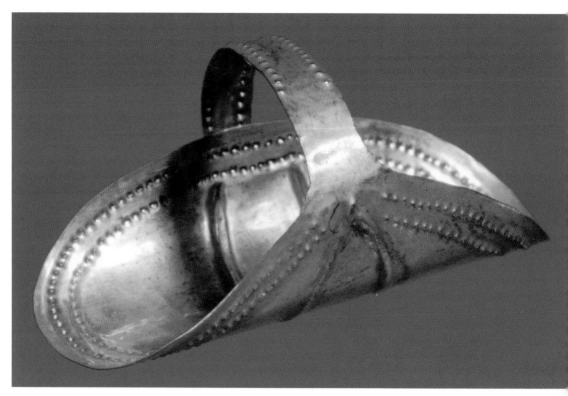

32 *The Kirkhaugh gold 'basket earring', or did it have some other ornamental use?*

Despite these obvious signs that people have used this area extensively in the past, the only signs of permanent occupation are two hillforts of a much later period.

We cannot say that the large Blawearie cairn is the largest or the richest in burials and grave goods in the region, because most of the others have not been investigated so thoroughly or even recorded. Some hints that others have included 'desirable' objects come from the collection made by a family of Blawearie shepherds, for this includes some fine jewellery of shale and jet as well as high quality flint implements (Newbigin, 1941).

This background sets one large cairn in a wider context, on a moor that has thin, poor soil unsuited to arable. It was lightly wooded in prehistoric times and provided good hunting or marginal pasture and water for stock.

Because the large cairn is so prominent it would have attracted the attention of treasure hunters. Fortunately, although the centre had been plundered before he arrived, Canon Greenwell at least brought some sort of ordered recording to what he found there, although this did not include a plan. His excavation took place on 2-3 August 1865. More recently the army used it in their training, and we found many spent blank cartridges buried in a shallow pit at the centre where Greenwell had reckoned a cist burial had been.

The excavation of the large cairn has revealed a complexity that is not surprising when compared to other recent excavations of cairns. The excavation of a mound, called Money Mound, in the Central Weald of Sussex, again with

81 *Blawearie excavation 1984: initial clearance.* Michael Ternouth

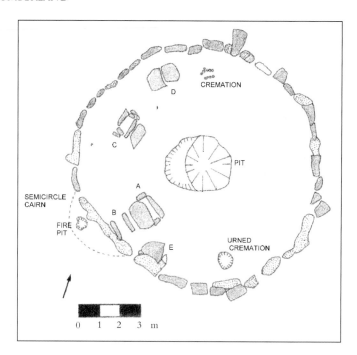

CREMATION
D

PIT

SEMICIRCLE
CAIRN

C

A

FIRE
PIT

B

E

URNED
CREMATION

0   1   2   3   m

82 *The main Blawearie*
cairn: selective plan

the involvement of young people, proved to have a similar history: a site ven-erated by later people, this time throughout the Roman occupation of Britain, disturbed in the eighteenth century, containing broken pieces of the original Beaker burial (Beckensall 1966).

Objects in the Blawearie mound fit an early Bronze Age date: a Food Vessel in a cist, an inverted Enlarged Food Vessel Urn, and a necklace of jet and shale beads. Some of the flint and single quartz artefacts did not come from the buri-als themselves and may represent activity in the general area before the mound was built. A knife from a cist pit and a burnt flint from a small circular pit filled with cremated bone and ash, and burnt flints from a cremation deposit in another cist are probably of the same period as the rest. The only metal object was a part of a copper ring from above the central pit.

Although these objects may cover roughly the same period, it was quite clear from the excavation that there was a sequence of events. The first phase was before the cairn was built. Dark organic soil in root cavities below the standing stones points to a tree being there, probably in the centre of the space occupied by the cairn. A layer of oak charcoal was spread across the centre of the cairn area, some of it perhaps from the burning of the tree. The removal of the stump may have been part of the digging of two conjoined pits which cut through the charcoal layers, one with vertical sides and the other shallower, reaching a large natural embedded boulder that made deeper digging more difficult. The deep-er pit had some vertical stones in the bottom, and may have housed a post. Both pits were backfilled with their own excavated material. This feature is not unusual in British barrows; pits and shafts were of significance to prehistoric people, just as caves were. An interesting discovery was a fossil cut into two equal parts, one at the bottom of the filled-in pit and the other at the top. At the very top of the pit in disturbed ground was part of a thin copper ring, perhaps connected with a cist burial with pottery that Greenwell recorded at the centre of the cairn, but we don't know for sure.

The filled pits became the centres of an ellipse of about 40 kerbstones that could have easily been quarried locally, for there are some outstanding outcrops nearby. They were erected either singly in individual pits or in groups in trenches. Upcast from the digging of these sockets and trenches mingled with the upcast from the central pits. As the sockets were shallow, some stones were shored up from the outside. Those stones chosen had triangular, flat or rounded tops. Some were tooled on their sides to make a comfortable fit. The space enclosed was then filled with cobbles and boulders that would have been lying around the moorland, including some ice-moved volcanic stones. They did not rise above the kerbstones. Throughout the construction of this ellipse of closely-fitting standing stones one may picture a group of people at work selecting suitable stones, hammering the edges with stone mauls, dragging the heavier stones along on sledges and levering them into their sockets. One kerbstone, later used as a cist cover, has notches that suggest it had ropes attached. When we came to reconstruct the mound, we encouraged our young people to work out a way of moving one of the large stones with levers and rollers, which they managed to do, but not without some argument. The use of planks beneath the rollers solved the major problem of how to move a flat stone without it sinking into excavated earth. At this stage the mound was a kerb circle, possibly with a cist or other burial at the centre.

Such a large circle then attracted secondary burials, all within two metres of the kerb. For the construction of cists, kerbstones were taken out or broken off, suggesting either that the very fabric was ritually important or that it was the easiest source of building material. The gaps made in the kerb enabled people to enter the mound, clear away cobbles and dig pits for the cist slabs. Once the cists had been made and the bodies or cremations buried, the circumference of the kerbs was made good, at one place being replaced by a small drystone wall. It was obviously important for the people to maintain the integrity of the monument.

There are very good examples of different kinds of cist construction. We labelled them cists A–E, and the way these graves differ is very interesting. A, dug by Greenwell, was a box of slabs slotted into the sides of a pit that was not dug through the natural base of the mound, but through upcast, and the sides of the cist were packed to stabilise it. Inside it was a Food Vessel with no body. The pointed covering slab fitted a socket to the west, from where it had most likely been moved with the help of ropes, as two notches suggest. The cist would then have been covered with a mixture of upcast and cobbles.

83-5 (Clockwise from top) *Cists A and B, with cist E behind; cist C; cist E*

B, also dug by Greenwell, had been cut through the upcast from Cist A, thus later than it. Made of two regular slabs running lengthways, it was set in a very shallow pit (which the diggers referred to as 'an economy job') with no end slabs or, at the time of discovery, slab cover. Inside was a jet and shale necklace and part of a flint knife; we found another half of a jet bead that Greenwell had missed from the same necklace. Again, the slabs, one pointed and the other tooled flat on one side, were reused kerbstones.

Close by this the edge of the cairn bulged into a small semicircular cairn which covered a small 'firepit' and rested on some of its upcast. It contained cremated human bone, oak charcoal and a small flint flake. Later than cist B, the digging of this pit and its filling may account for the fact that part of that cist is missing.

Cist C had been excavated by Greenwell and declared empty. Because the soil is acidic the bones of any original burial may not have survived. It is rectangular like the others, but instead of having single end-slabs, this had two at each end. We thoroughly excavated this cist, revealing the packing stones around the box. Again the cist cover was a reused kerbstone, with very clear tool markings where it had been prepared to fit snugly against another. The wall outside this had a snapped-off kerbstone and a kerbstone on either side had been removed. The resulting gap was filled with a drystone wall.

Greenwell had missed cist D. Lying underneath piles of cobbles, it had two capstones over an elliptical arrangement of vertical and horizontal stones, sunk in a pit and surrounded by upcast. Tests on a dark stain inside the cist for traces of a buried body were inconclusive, and the nest of a small animal inside the cist suggested that the soil had been contaminated. It was above the capstones of this cist where a blue glass melon bead was found, looking as fresh as the day it was made.

Cist E, again missed by Greenwell, was constructed in a pit that had been dug after two kerbs had been removed. Because the upcast from the pit overlay that of cist A, it had been constructed later. The cist slabs were skilfully arranged, and held in position from the inside by packed upcast that contained a cremation deposit of an adult and child accompanied by five burnt flints. The top of the cist was levelled with small stones, a large slab covered it, and the whole was covered with upcast and cobbles.

These five cists, all added at different times, and the small fire pit were not the end of the story. Close to cist D an area of cobbles had been removed, and nine small cobbles had been arranged in a roughly rectangular shape; a cremation of an adult mixed with soil was inserted. It was capped with a small slab and buried with cobbles. Finally, a small pit was dug through upcast and the natural base of the mound to the south for an inverted urn that contained some burnt remains of two men. The bones had been inserted after the urn had been turned upside down and the bottom broken off to admit them. The base was replaced, covered with a slab, and earth and cobbles sealed it all in.

Many different individual burials inserted at different times are not a rarity in British barrows; the sequencing of these and the different methods of treatment, such as cremation, inhumation, the presence or absence of grave goods and of their type are of great interest. An outstanding feature of the use of the site itself is that from the beginning the circular arrangement of the ritual area was respected, and that the reuse of existing kerbstones for the construction of cists was important to that ritual. The continuing veneration of the site may be represented by the burying of the blue melon bead; it is possible that the amber necklace may be later too, although its closeness to cist A and the centre could mean that it had been dug out unnoticed at some early time.

86 *Blawearie satellite cairns under excavation*

That is not the end of the story; not only is the mound a cemetery; it is the focus of many other small cairns that lie to the east, and on the slopes leading down to the bridle path and beyond in the flat, rather marshy area. The latter includes a kerbed cairn that we re-excavated because it had been dug at the centre, but it produced no artefacts. The rest were recorded without being excavated.

We excavated two satellite cairns to the east of the large mound. One had a kerb of stones larger than the cobbles that it enclosed, covering a pit that had burnt soil, charcoal and cremated bone. The deposit was covered with a polygonal arrangement of small flat stones capped with a slab, making it look like a cist without being one. The other, smaller, cairn was a circle of stones, some embedded vertically, with no pit and no organic remains. It cannot be classed as a 'burial', but its kerbed structure echoes that of all the other cairns in the area.

What about the people? It seems that the primary use of the area was for hunting and herding; the only traces of early fields are on Hepburn Hill close to a cluster of burial mounds. Pollen samples from the Blawearie excavation suggest moorland that was partly open, partly wooded with mainly hazel, birch and alder. The oak charcoal at the centre of the barrow may belong to the remnants of earlier woodland that had more oak trees. Oak may have been of special significance, as the cremations included fragments of oak charcoal.

The reasons for burying people with ornaments, pottery and implements can only be guessed. A jet and shale necklace and an amber necklace are rare and valuable, so why take them out of circulation by burying them? The jet, possibly from the Whitby area, is undamaged. The amber necklace has countersunk holes so that the beads could fit together well; the pendant bead was almost worn

87 *Satellite cairns reinstated. Left to itself, heather has grown in the soil since 1988*

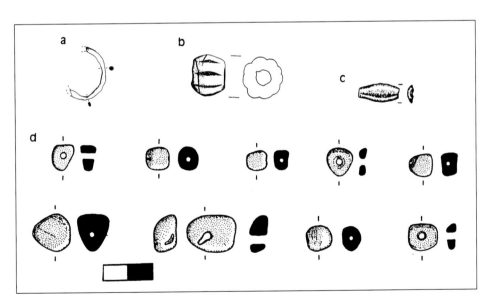

88 *Blawearie finds: a) copper ring, b) melon blue glass bead, c) jet bead, d) nine amber beads.* British Museum

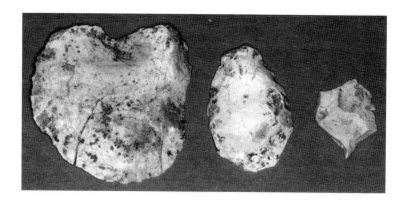

89 *Flints from cist E, part of the cremation of an adult and child.* Dr I. Macleod

through from its hole to the circumference, suggesting that it had been around someone's neck for a long time. We cannot assign either to man, woman or child. They're unlikely to serve the same purpose as the shaman's kit mentioned above. Perhaps they were buried because no one could bear the thought of anyone else wearing them. Perhaps the family line had died out. Perhaps no one else was worthy to inherit them. Another possibility is that people believed in some sort of afterlife when the necklaces would re-emerge. Pottery might be an attractive gift to link the living with the dead, a reminder of life on earth. As flint implements belong to the work-a-day world, they too would be important reminders of the everyday world. The burnt flints have changed their nature in fire. Those in cist E are of the type that were used for cutting and scraping out animal skins so that they could be pegged out and dried.

At Blawearie there are two distinct methods of disposing of the dead: inhumation and cremation. It seems unlikely that people would go to the trouble of making a cist without putting a body in it, but we still build memorials when the body is not available for burial. The soil is acidic, and unburned human bones can disappear completely. Cist E, however, contained the burnt remains of an adult and child who had been cremated outside the cairn, allowed to go cold, and brought in a bag for the burial, and the cremated remains survive. The fire pit and the cremation in the satellite cairn were either burnt on the spot or brought in hot, for the soil in the pits had been burnt. The two males in the inverted urn had not been thoroughly cremated like the others, and their remains represented only a part of the bodies. How was the selection made for burial? What happened to the rest of them?

It is not unusual to find cremation and inhumation burials taking place at the same time, even in the same grave, in the early Bronze Age. Later, cremation becomes the norm. Whatever method was used, it was important to bury the remains, cover them over whether it be in cist or pit. There is something very firm and final about cist burials, capping them with a heavy slab. Could it be telling them to stay where they were? The cairn above them was a visible monument that people using the area would have recognised, which might attract later people to bury votive offerings there or insert a later burial. Sadly it might also attract treasure hunters. The blue melon bead may be accounted for as a votive offering, perhaps the amber necklace too, although this might have been disturbed from its place within the mound by diggers. In the highlands of Scotland there was a recent tradition of people adding stones to cairns on occasions like anniversaries.

To refer again to Money Mound, this is a classic site for evidence of votive offerings, with many types of Iron Age and Romano-British pottery, beads and coins. Although its earliest artefacts were Mesolithic, these could have been incorporated in soils scooped up to form the centre of the barrow. Flints at Blawearie could have preceded the building of the mound, too. The primary purpose of Money Mound was as a Beaker grave, the pottery being accompanied by two equal barbed and tanged arrowheads. It also had three copper rivets that belonged to a knife similar to one found in a cist at Allerwash (see below).

There is no doubt that Greenwell's excavation methods were such that he missed much. He did not locate the 'natural' base of the mound, did not dig deeply enough, and his trenching was based on the assumption that it was not necessary to remove the north and west sides of a mound 'as they are generally found to be destitute of secondary interments' (1877). His work was also very patchy, but this is not surprising when we realise that he spent only two days on the site. We spent five seasons, about eight weeks, with a much bigger labour force than he had available.

90 *A massive capstone and cist at the centre of a large disturbed cairn north of the Harehope Burn*

The significance of the Blawearie cairns in the landscape will only be understood if more work is undertaken in a much wider area, including selective excavation. The first step is to record all the cairns that have not yet appeared on a map.

91 *A decorated slab among a cluster of cairns*

92 *A cairn focused on a standing stone north of the Harehope Burn*

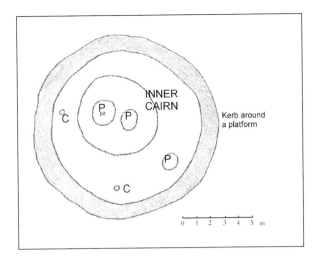

93 *Chatton Sandyford cairn: main features. P = pit; C = cremation.* Based on G. Jobey

Chatton Sandyford (Jobey, 1969)

The late Professor George Jobey excavated cairns at Chatton Sandyford that make very interesting comparisons and contrasts with the Blawearie cairns. The site is in a remote area where there is little human activity today, apart from forestry and some animal husbandry. The cairnfield itself has two large cairns and 150 small ones, most of which have been disturbed. They extend along the flat crest of a ridge for about three-quarters of a mile from north to south. Recently I have recorded cup- and ring-marked slabs among these cairns (Beckensall 2001b, 142-3) at Whitehill Head. Although the land is largely stone-free and smooth, as though for farming, no early field systems have been found, so, as with Blawearie, we are left wondering where the people who are buried here lived. Like Blawearie, there are extensive views from the cairns, reaching the sea.

Jobey excavated the site in 1965/6, but an outbreak of foot and mouth disease curtailed the excavations, though not before he had produced some impressive results. On some old OS maps the site of the large cairn that he excavated was called 'Camp'; it looked like a small walled enclosure before excavation, 12.9m (40ft) in diameter, and 0.91m (3ft) high. Like Blawearie, it showed disturbance at the centre and part of the kerb, but there was no record of previous digging. Some of the stone from the mound had been used to make enclosures abutting it.

The site was quartered for excavation. The story of its history was revealed, of course, in reverse order during the excavation; what now follows begins at the beginning.

When cairns are built, the area may be first cleared of vegetation to create a space. As the cairn is to be built of stone, this can either be quarried or picked off the land surface as boulders or cobbles. Perhaps these were piled up in readiness while the grave was prepared. The first burial was an inhumation in a shallow, oval grave 1.52m (5ft) x 1.30m (4ft 3in) and only 0.25m (10in) deep. As the soil is acidic, no trace of a body survived. Although the grave was superficially robbed, a crushed Beaker remained against a lining of undisturbed weathered sandstones. Two V-shaped jet buttons came from the disturbed material outside the grave. When the upcast was moved out of the pit to make the grave a large columnar piece of sandstone was put in a socket vertically to act as a grave marker. West of this grave was a patch of burning and charcoal, and there were four driven stake holes with the burnt points still at the bottom. All the charcoal was oak, as we found at Blawearie; the use of this wood may have been of significance on both sites, as it was not the common wood in areas such as these. It was dated to 1670±50 BC. The significance at Chatton Sandyford is that this wood was possibly used in the actual cremation on the spot.

Shortly after the first, a second burial took place, which somehow escaped the robbers. It was a circular pit 1.83m (6ft) in diameter, 1.52m (5ft) deep, with near vertical sides. Again the body was buried uncremated; at the bottom lay a cracked but complete Beaker. The pit was filled with its own upcast and covered with a low mound.

Both of these burials were then covered with large stones that formed the base of a mound, some picked off the land and others split off outcrop, leaning against each other, tilted inwards from the centre outwards. At this stage the mound was smaller than the one we see today. Another inhumation and Beaker were added in an oval-shaped pit 1.37m (4ft 6in) long and 1.02m (3ft 4in) deep. The upcast was raked over it. Robbers smashed the Beaker, but left some fragments. They threw two large stones into the grave that had come from the next feature to be described.

The mound that had covered the early graves ('a monument in its own right') was extended by the construction of a kerb, about 0.61-0.91m (2ft-3ft) outside the mound. People dug a trench through the subsoil, cut slabs of stone and erected them against the outer face of this trench. To make sure that the kerbstones fitted against each other closely the builders pecked the sides to make a tight fit. We have seen the same principle at Blawearie, but there the kerbstones were chunkier and less regular, and they were not all placed in a continuous trench. At both sites the sockets and trench were packed tight. Many of the stones were 0.91m (3ft) high and up to 0.31 (1ft) thick. The circle (as at Blawearie) was not perfect; in some sections it ran in short straight lengths. The chippings from the shaping of the kerbs were found in the cairn and some in the packing along with weathered stone cobbles taken from the surface of the surrounding land. Inside this kerb circle a platform made of stones capped with compact light sandy soil was constructed 0.91m (3ft) wide. This amazing feature surrounded the large stones that were the boundaries of the earlier cairn. The robbers threw two of these new kerbs into the

94 *Chatton Sandyford cairn.* J. Tait, NUM

burial pit described above; they had the distinctive pick markings on them. They had been removed to allow the robbers to break into the centre of the cairn. At Blawearie the removal of kerbs had a different purpose: to enable prehistoric people to add to the burials in the 'sacred' area and then to complete the circle again.

The excavator was not sure whether the third burial took place at the same time as the laying down of the kerbstones or before it. There were two more prehistoric burials to come, between the first mound and the kerb and platform. One cremation in an Enlarged Food Vessel lay over two base stones. Near it lay a large columnar block of pitted limestone, a grave marker again. Near this was a cup-marked stone: there were five complete cups on one side and one that was cut through, showing that it had probably been broken from a larger piece. On the opposite side were four faint cups, unfinished.

A second cremation was unurned; this one had probably been brought in a bag and was inserted between the upper edges of two base stones. There were eight multi-purpose flint tools found in the mound, which could have been on the surface before the mound was built or deliberately included in it.

Finally, there were seven fragments of a Roman flagon that may have come from a disturbed Roman burial inserted in the mound. Money Mound offers parallels.

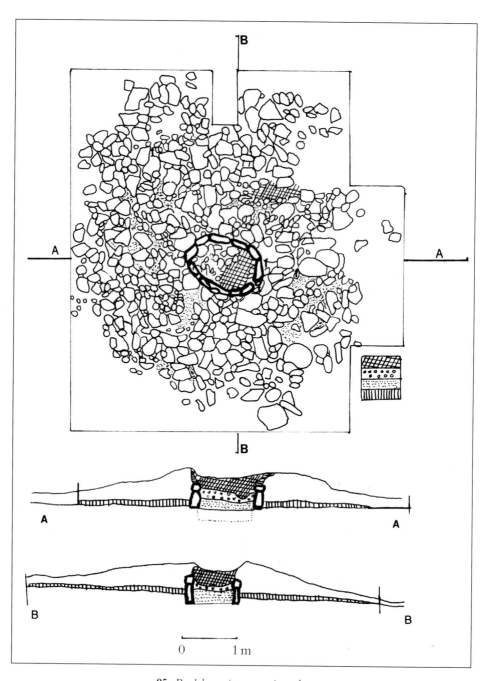

95 *Brockdam cairn excavation: plans.*
Layers, top to bottom: disturbed soil and stone; disturbed soil; compacted sand; brown stained soil

The exploration of some small cairns in the same area and at the same time draws attention to a problem of what kind of mounds these might be. There are about 150 of them, some of which may have been for burial, but others might be field clearance heaps. None of the five investigated had burials or grave goods, and one produced a surprising date of 2890 BC. This date could be the result of some very early material being incorporated in a pile of stones; it can only be earlier than the cairn building or contemporary with it, but how much earlier? Although many, like the large mound, have been opened by robbers, there will be plenty of new information awaiting the skilled excavator.

Other examples of early Bronze Age burial places

It is impossible to do more than select a few sites for description and discussion; this will illustrate the breadth of the subject.

Among recent excavations of cairns in Northumberland is one at Brockdam. It stands on a ridge overlooking the A1, Tynely, Ellingham and the sea to the east. Before excavation it was a grassed mound with a sagging pit on top at the centre. The bowl-shaped arrangement of stones covered a single central cist that had been robbed. There was no sign of a cover, but the oval-shaped arrangement of small vertical stones that formed the robbed cist sur-

96 Brockdam: the reinstated cairn with a central cist

97 *Brockdam cairn: central oval cist*

vived. Whatever it contained had been lifted out without much disturbance, but we shall never know what was found there. The pit in the mound must then have been roughly filled with excavated material. During our excavation we examined all the cobbles to see if any were marked, and rebuilt the cairn around the cist, now filled with gravel to stabilise it.

At Weetwood and Fowberry three cairns that I have described in detail elsewhere (Beckensall 2002) (NU 0215 2810, 0155 2840, 0197 2784) are special in that they are partly built of cobbles that have prehistoric motifs pecked onto them. The Fowberry cairn is built on a large ridge of outcrop rock that is covered with motifs. Here we have mound-building deliberately incorporating rock art, and the design on a large kerb boulder of the Weetwood mound is echoed by one pecked out on an outcrop not far away (Whitsun Bank). There are increasingly more examples of mound sites where rock art is included. The problem with mounds, however, is that they may have been so disturbed that there is no sign of a burial, so we cannot assume that burial was always their purpose. In Northumberland, in County Durham, Swaledale and Wensleydale, many such mounds directly associated with rock art have now been recorded. An excavation of a cist at Witton Gilbert near Durham city is particularly important, as this has produced pristine rock art along with cremation dated to about 2000 BC (Beck, 1999).

Not all burials are accompanied by grave goods. At Howick in 2002, the excavation of five cists on the same site as Mesolithic material, revealed that these cists were constructed from easily-carried stone slabs, some shale, from the beach to line graves that bore no trace of human remains or of any artefacts (Waddington forthcoming). Whether they were covered with cairns and presented some sort of visual impact to seafarers is doubtful. They are impor-

98 *The Fowberry mound, built on a long outcrop of decorated rock*

99 *Howick, 2002: early Bronze Age cist*

tant discoveries, especially when added to the Low Hauxley (NU 294 018) burials to the south, where storms in 1983 and 1994 revealed cists, some with cremations and others with crouched skeletons (Hardie 2000). There is some evidence that these cists were covered with cairns. These bodies were buried with a Beaker and flint knife. One of the cists has been removed from its original position and reconstructed at the Low Hauxley Nature Reserve.

The barrows and rock shelters reported here are all at significant viewpoints, the places deliberately chosen because they could be seen from a distance. There are other burials within a setting of standing stones. At Duddo and Goatstones (see below) the standing stones surround what appears to have been a pit containing cremation in each case. Small and large single standing stones are present in some barrows: a small one at Lordenshaw (NZ 0557 9942), for example, and a large one in a barrow in the Harehope Burn valley, Old Bewick Hill.

Prehistoric burials are sometimes revealed by accidental disturbance of the earth where there is nothing to see on the surface. At Cartington (NU 037 053) (Dixon, 1903) near Rothbury, a prehistoric tree-trunk coffin was found over one hundred years ago. It was reported to contain an inhumation laid on bracken accompanied by flints, some leather fragments and what appears to have been a Beaker. Further south, more recently a burial was excavated at Allerwash (Newman 1976), near Haydon Bridge. Located on a gravel knoll on the north side of the Tyne, it was discovered when a deep plough hit the cist cover. Inside were fragments of a young girl who had been laid on a bed of rushes. She was buried with a bronze dagger with three rivets for the handle. This dated the burial to around 2000 BC. The cist in which she lay was made of three slabs packed into the pit, the gaps sealed with clay, the spaces around it packed with upcast, the top levelled off and the cover slab placed over it.

There was another burial at Altonside, Haydon Bridge (NY 856 649), in a very nice cist with a Beaker, but no skeleton survived (Jobey 1978). Further east along the Tyne at Dilston three cists that were not covered with mounds produced an inhumation, a cremated adolescent with three Beakers in one cist and another cremation with two Beakers.

More recently a new type of burial structure has been recognised: the tri-radial cairn (see chapter 4). This is a meeting of three walls of stone at a common centre, rather like a Mercedes car logo. During a widespread recording and excavation of sites in the Cheviot Hills at Ingram the first of these appeared on a hill overlooking the valley. Since this discovery, others have been identified. At Lordenshaw, south of the fort and the hollow way leading up to it, is a distinctive tri-radial cairn, pictured here, that has not been further investigated. It was probably overlooked because its shape could have been attributed to field walls that cross, but this is not the case. The cairn is detached from such walls.

Another area of discovery has been at Ray Sunniside (Ford 2002), where the Borders Archaeological Society, led by Bill Ford of Newcastle University, excavated a cairn that was almost buried (NY 9581 8491). It lay on a ridge covered with multi-period earthworks, hut circles and cairns; the tri-radial lay on the southern edge of a group of twenty cairns. Unlike the Turf Knowe cairn, which was made up of parallel walls of large boulders packed with smaller stones, this one had the large stones placed centrally in the three walls. Unlike Turf Knowe, no burials were found, but a carbon date of 2648-2636 BC gave its earliest date of construction, which appears to be earlier than that at Turf Knowe. The concentration of stone at the place where the three arms met and the alignment of the arms made it similar to others that the group has found (true north, 140 and 240 degrees being the general alignments). The group believes that the excavated cairn gave the approximate directions of sun-

100 *Lordenshaw: tri-radial cairn south of the hillfort*

rise and sunset on Midsummer Day, and that the sightings along the south-east and south-west arms gave the approximate direction of sunrise and sunset at midwinter. An important find was a cup-marked stone built into the south-east arm. There are two other tri-radial cairns there, one with a cup mark.

One interesting example of the continuity of use of a burial site is at West Hepple (NT 975 007). In 1972 Roger Miket excavated the site of a destroyed chapel that had very wide, uninterrupted views in many directions (Miket, 1974). The site had already revealed a Bronze Age cremation in 1821: 'several urns have been found' in 'small barrows thrown up over the kistvaens. About eight of them in all' (Hodgson). Also a jet bead was found by Greenwell with a buried body in a cairn near Hepple and a miniature Food Vessel (both now in the British Museum). When the graveyard and chapel, then a raised grass platform, were excavated it was found that stone had been taken away and burials dispersed. Underneath the site of Christian burials were prehistoric flints, but it was the excavation of two pit burials that claimed attention. One was south of the possible church entrance: an inverted collared urn in a rough ovoid pit, filled with material that showed signs of burning, and containing at least three adults and a child. Another pit was under the west nave wall, probably of the same date and origin, but with no pottery or bone. It is interesting that the site continued in use as a simple nave and chancel, with a graveyard.

The early Bronze Age was the most prolific time for cairns. After that the sites were still revered, and further burials could be inserted in mounds that retained their sanctity. Votive offerings continued to be made in the Iron Age and Roman period. In parts of Britain, Saxon high-status burials focused on

101 *The Hepple urn, covered with the original stone cap.* NUM

some of these early sites, such as the Milfield Plain henges and at Yeavering, with its whole focus on a Bronze Age cemetery.

In parts of southern and central England barrows continued to attract later deposits, when flat cremation cemeteries became the normal method of burying the dead from about 1200-900 BC. People were reluctant to bury expensive grave goods with them. All over the country after 1500 BC cremation became the norm. The type of pottery that contained the cremations changed to large coarse pots and urns that were probably the same as those used for domestic cooking; styles varied in different parts of the country.

Very little is known of burial practice or ceremonial monuments from the middle Bronze Age onwards. Clearly the dead were disposed of in ways that leave few traces in the archaeological record. Paul Frodsham thinks that on balance there is a strong possibility that cremations were scattered on fields or placed within field boundaries. The fields were of ritual significance to people as well as providing them with their food. Further investigation may in due course support or refute this. Another possibility is that people were disposed of in rivers, lakes, bogs, and other wet places (Frodsham 2000).

Cairns are the most common repositories for dead prehistoric people, but there are other places where the dead were buried. Two rock shelters have burials in their floors: at Goatscrag Hill and at Corby's Crags. Both have been excavated using modern methods.

Goatscrag Hill (NT 976 371) rises from a long ridge on which there are panels of rock art, and where there were recorded burial mounds, now destroyed. The crag faces the Broomridgedean valley, a route to the Milfield

Plain, and along the scarp are rock overhangs, exposing attractive layers of many-coloured sedimentary rock. On the overhang of one of these shelters are unusual motifs of pairs of cups joined by curved grooves, like horseshoes. On the vertical wall of the largest shelter is a group of four animal figures, three static and one running. They appear to be old, perhaps pictures of deer or goats, but cannot be dated.

The largest rock shelter was excavated by Colin Burgess (1972), and proved to be an early Bronze Age cemetery: two cremation burials were in attractive Enlarged Food Vessels, and there were two others that were unurned. There were many pits and post holes, indicating some sort of ritual connected with them. A second overhang had a number of rock-cut pits, and both shelters had many flints that are not necessarily connected with the burials. Such overhangs were ideal for temporary shelter where flint tools and arrows could be manufactured. There were also some pieces of modern china in the topsoil, clay pipe fragments and three joining sherds of medieval pottery. Some pits formed a line along the face of the overhang, and could have been for some sort of screen. One pit in the floor (a 'fire pit') had near-vertical sides and a flat bottom, and was filled with mainly birch charcoal and cremated bone. There was another pit cremation. An inverted cinerary urn had been sunk into a tight pit. With the lower half broken cleanly off, it was found that the pot had been broken by the people burying it, the sherds were carefully placed on the burnt bones inside the pot, and then covered with sand. The remains proved to be those of a young adult male. Only a metre away from this was a pit with vertical sides and flat bottom with cremated bone and a burnt flint flake.

The second urned burial was inverted and unbroken, with a flat stone placed over it, covered with sand. It lay on the natural base. The urn was packed with the poorly cremated remains of a young adult and a young child aged about two, possibly a mother and child.

102 *Detail of Goatscrag excavated Food Vessel containing human cremation*

The third burial was found covered with a thin slab, the cremation of a young adult being on the natural base, accompanied by half a barrel-shaped bead made of lignite and a large flint flake. Most flints found during the excavation could be of any period, but there were two Mesolithic blades on the undisturbed subsoil, the earliest period of use of this shelter.

There is another very important rock shelter at Ketley Crag, Chatton Park Hill (NU 0743 2978), the floor of which is covered with some of the most attractive rock art in Britain. Its exposure is recent, but there was no sign of any burial on the floor (Beckensall 2001). Bearing in mind the two shelters just described, one may only surmise that a body could have been laid on the decorated floor. Like the other sites, this one has fabulous views from it. It also lies in an area where there is high quality rock art nearby and some small enclosures. These rock shelters, with their dominating position in the landscape, their use throughout prehistory, the coincidence of all of them with rock art and the use of two of them for burial gives them a unique place in archaeology. Near Rothbury, Cartington Cove (NU 0444 0186), reported as having rock art, was blown up by quarrying. Another, at Doddington, is known as 'Cuddy's Cave' (NU 00360 31010), in which cups and rings were recorded but have now gone. This 'cave' is traditionally one of the places where the body of St Cuthbert was laid down for a while on its journeys around the north to escape the attention of the Vikings. The body now lies in Durham cathedral.

103 *Ketley Crag: the decorated rock shelter floor*

6

PREHISTORIC ROCK ART

Readers who are familiar with rock art in other parts of the world may be aware that images pecked or painted onto rocks include a high proportion of pictures of people, animals and human activities. During my first visit to southern Sweden in 2002 I was impressed by pictures of boats, horses and chariots, ploughs being pulled by oxen, and weapons. Such images are not merely pictures, however, as their frequent appearance suggests that they were charged with a special meaning. This undercurrent of meaning that may elude us today was reinforced by the number of cup marks, sandaled and bare feet petrified as they walked down the rock, spirals and serpentine grooves. On one rock was a powerful dancing figure occupying its own unique place, drawing attention to its own special nature.

Northumberland and other places in Britain have patterns that consist of abstract symbols. Cup and ring marks are what they have been called since they were discovered; the term is appropriate, for a cup and ringed groove are two essential elements in most compositions. From this very simple beginning, an arrangement of the symbols results at best in designs that take into account the natural surface of the rock and its place in the landscape, actually enhancing that rock and stressing its importance. The people who used a hard stone tool to peck these symbols onto rocks in widespread concentrations in north Britain clearly had a similar vocabulary, but the skill with which they arranged the symbols on the rocks to create designs shows that some people were more articulate than others.

Northumberland has played, and continues to play, a crucial role in the study of these markings, in attempts to understand who put them there, when and why. The 1820s saw the first discovery made at Old Bewick Hill, when John Charles Langlands recognised the marks as being 'ancient' and important rather than the work of an idle shepherd. Since then many interested people, notably amateur historians with skills that included medicine, law, theology and education, have searched for new sites and for explanations.

Northumberland has always been to the fore in this research. Only recently has rock art been taken seriously as a vital part of prehistory. It is no longer enough to record the designs; we now look at its distribution in the landscape

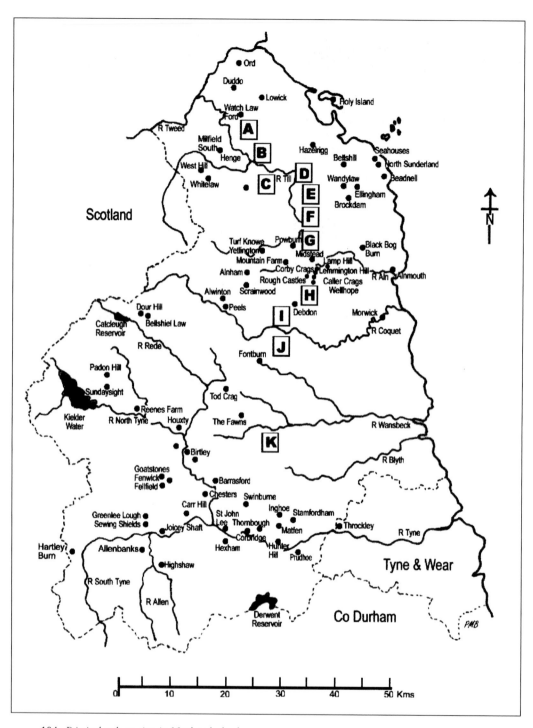

104 *Principal rock art sites in Northumberland.*
A: Broomridge, Roughting Linn, Hare Crags; B: Doddington; C: Weetwood, Fowberry, Lilburn;
D: Chatton Park Hill; E: Amerside Law, Ros Castle, Chatton Sandyford; F: Hepburn, Old Bewick;
G: Beanley, Hunterheugh; H: Millstone Burn, Snook Bank; I: Cartington, Chirnells Moor;
J: Lordenshaw; K: Wallington, Middleton Bank, Shaftoe, Shortflatt. Paul Brown

105 (Above) *Old Bewick: the first designs to be recognised as ancient.* Birtley Aris

106 (Right) *Collingwood Bruce's lithograph*

and ask what it is doing there, and why some rocks rather than others were singled out for this special treatment. We look at its position in burials and monuments and ask the same questions. I and other researchers look also for *portable* examples, rocks taken away from their original sites and either dumped or built into structures such as field and house walls.

What now follows is a summary of the extensive work that I published in *Prehistoric Rock Art in Northumberland* (2001). All sites mentioned below are detailed in that book.

Art in the landscape

In the landscape the decorated outcrop rocks occupy high ground overlooking valleys, suggesting trails, migratory routes, good viewpoints. They probably belong to early agriculturalists whose lifestyle was still partly nomadic, for pastoralism and hunting outside the settlements were important activities in the search for food and material for clothes. Their bases were now fixed with fields, walls and houses in the most fertile areas.

Sometimes the marked rocks are at the highest part of the landscape; at Chatton Park Hill, for example, there are extensive stretches of fairly smooth outcrop that are ideal for this kind of art, but the part chosen for the most spectacular motifs is the highest. Others may not be so high in the landscape, but the views from them are wide-ranging. The largest decorated panel looks across the valley of the River Till to the west, its course already marked by panels for much of its course as it flows towards the threshold where the river

107 *Chatton Park Hill: part of the main panel (2001)*

breaks through a scarp to meet the Milfield Plain, already seen as an important settlement and ritual centre in Neolithic and later times. Although the nature of a 'viewpoint' depends on whether or not the land around the marked rocks was wooded, this large rock would not have been surrounded by trees. The outcrop at the edge of the scarp had to be exposed from the beginning before it could be marked; trees could not have grown on or around it in this case. Further north along the same ridge a defended settlement is centred on a patch of outcrop that was marked before the fort was built.

The largest decorated surface of outcrop rock in England is at Roughting Linn (Twohig 1988), a whaleback of sandstone now partly quarried away, with many variations on the cup and ring theme. It is part of a scatter of rock art that continues through Goatscrag Hill and Broomridge westward along the sandstone scarp towards the Milfield Plain. The whaleback is one sign of pre-historic activity; the promontory to which it leads is cut off and defended by a number of concentric ditches and walls that form an undated enclosure. In addition to the scarp itself as a ridgeway, there is an old track with a modern surface, partly hollow way, that heads west to an entrance to the Milfield Plain. The rock art concentrates on the edges of the whaleback, reminding some of the way in which the Irish passage grave kerbstones are decorated on the out-side of the mound. The idea of marking the rock may have been suggested by the pattern of natural erosion to the north, where even the roughest parts have

108 *Roughting Linn: facing north-east*

109 *Roughting Linn: facing east*

been added to with grooves and cups and rings. The natural rock slopes are followed by grooves leading from cups at the centre of rings.

This and sites at Weetwood Moor, Dod Law and Old Bewick are among the easiest of access and the most interesting in the north of the County, and appear on OS maps.

Northumberland has a unique location for rock art in its rock shelters; some are associated with burials (see above), but one at Ketley Crag on Chatton Park Hill has one of the finest designs in Britain. Without rock art the crag may have been a prominent landscape feature; it must be remembered that before land was cleared and farmed that prominent natural features may have been essential to find one's way across country. Some had their prominence enhanced by marking them, as in the case of the cliffs at Morwick or the table of rock at Old Bewick. The floor of the Ketley Crag rock overhang was fully decorated, using every subtle variation on its surface to guide the mason's design. Indeed, this is one of the finest examples anywhere. It is overlooked by other rock art to the south, this time on a small plateau of outcrop.

It could be that the choice of a rock surface for marking had many explanations. In parts of Britain I have observed how some decorated surfaces mark springs, and do not command extensive views. Others may commemorate events now lost to us, perhaps where an act of bravery, humour of tragedy took place. If the markings were serious enough to be buried with the dead, they would have carried a powerful message for those who encountered them. What we shall not learn, however, is how the symbols originated, what they meant to the people who used them, or precisely when they were made. We assume their currency to be over a thousand years; it is possible that people for-

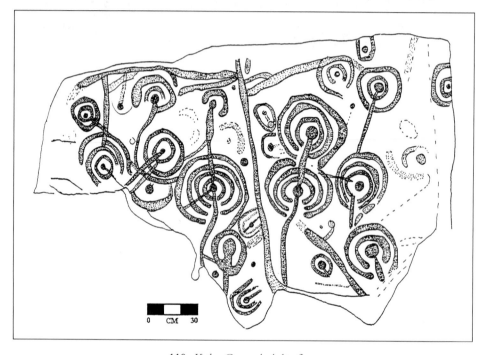

110 *Ketley Crag rock shelter floor*

111 *Rosettes from Doddington Moor*

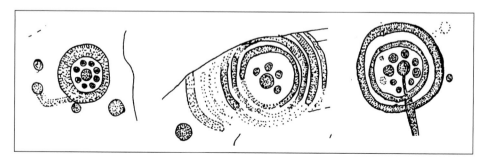

112 *Dod Law main rock*

got everything about them except that these were the marks that were made to commemorate an event. The meaning and use no doubt changed over time.

There is, for all the frustration of not knowing answers to fundamental questions, a potency about these symbols that enables us to admire them. It is remarkable how many variations on a theme the makers managed to achieve. We do not have to look for sources of inspiration that lie outside the human brain, for the desire to incorporate circles into art and into the plans of buildings is strong. To 'invent' a rosette design for example, the person who discovered it in Northumberland did not have to know someone in Ormaig (Argyll). Indeed the similarities between cups and rings and similar patterns all over the world make sense when we realise that the circle is a simple but potent symbol among many people. It makes sense, however, to look for similarities in designs within a region; thus we see that there are individual touches: multiple radial grooves at Dod Law and Weetwood, rosettes at Dod Law and Hare Law Crags, or squares and heart shapes at Dod Law, Amersidelaw Moor and Chatton Park Hill. Did the same group make them? We don't know, but it is possible.

Art in monuments

The decorated floor of the Ketley Crag rock overhang and the spirals on the cliff at Morwick enhance prominent features that already make them special places; when this is combined with burial it makes them even more special. The Corby's Crag rock shelter cremation burial and the burials under the over-

113 *Fowberry*

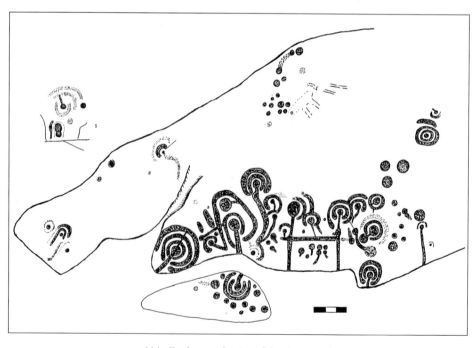

114 *Fowberry – drawing of the above panel*

hang at Goatscrag Hill already described in this book combined with the decoration mean that the sites were special for two reasons. Whether burials and markings occur at the same time cannot be proved, but this is likely. Mounds that contain rock art in their structure add another context.

The excavated mound at Weetwood incorporated many decorated cobbles and a large boulder that had faced inward into the mound as a kerbstone (Beckensall 2001b). The excavation of nearby Fowberry (Beckensall 2001b) revealed a double-kerbed cairn with over twenty decorated cobble stones lying on a long stretch of outcrop that was covered with motifs sensitive to the nature of that rock. Stones in Berwick Museum and the Museum of Antiquities at Newcastle taken from late Neolithic/early Bronze Age mounds show that the rock art, instead of being a part of the landscape, open to the skies and enhancing it, were now buried face down in a burial context; a quite different use. Recently many cup marked stones have been found among cairns and within the cairn structures; the excavation of a selected few of such sites might provide more links between burial and the motifs. Cup marks also appear on standing stones, such as Duddo or Matfen, and a four-poster burial site at Goatstones has cup marks on the tops of the stones. A cup-marked stone came from a pit in a henge on the Milfield Plain.

If it were not for the rock art being in or on monuments it would be impossible to date it as yet, and its presence there ties it to a use from about 4-5,000 years ago. At Dod Law the excavation of the hillfort annex (see above) shows that the Iron Age structures overlie the cup- and ring-marked outcrops, but that does not give us a precise date (only pre-approx. 500 BC). Neither must we rely solely on Northumberland's discoveries, for all British sites have to be considered together.

The most important recent excavation of a cist that included cremations and rock art is at Fulforth Farm, Durham. The cover slab was decorated on two sides, the more elaborate face-downward into the cist, and two pristine decorated panels were incorporated into the cist construction. Unfortunately, the report has not yet been fully published, but the contents of the cist are known to be late Neolithic/early Bronze Age. The future of rock art study must include more excavation of promising sites that can tell us much more than we know already about context and date.

Portable rock art

It is obvious that much rock art has been destroyed, by quarrying, for example. There are many 'portable' examples of rock art in the field and in museums, but one rock at Newcastle deserves special mention. From Lilburn, it came out of a grave pit, probably Neolithic, which contained cremations accompanied by a triangular-shaped stone with horned spiral and concentric rings. The cremations were reported to have been in a pit in two layers, each individual deposit covered with small pieces of whinstone. Portable examples that find their way into field-clearance heaps, house walls, field walls and rockeries may be from destroyed monuments. The church of St John Lee, near Hexham, for example, houses a well-decorated slab picked off the ridge nearby. At Corbridge Roman site and at Prudhoe Castle are two further fine examples.

In the middle and south of the county the best sites to visit include Lordenshaw, within the National Park and well signposted, which includes a great variety of rock art styles and cairns that have motifs included, or which stand on decorated outcrop. One of the most intriguing sites, though not so accessible, has been mentioned: Morwick Mill, Warkworth, where a cliff face rising from the River Coquet is covered with unique spiral motifs.

115 *Lilburn: a decorated slab from a pit grave with multiple cremations.* NUM

116 *St John Lee church (Hexham): a replica made by John Price*

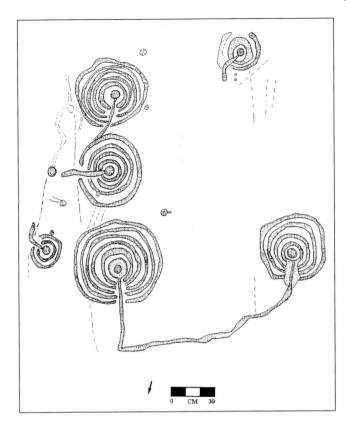

117 *Weetwood (left) and Stamfordham (above), the latter in Alnwick Castle Museum*

The best rock art has been saved from destruction because it lies in areas that were not particularly good for cereal crops, but good for hunting and pasture. Portable examples may point to a wider distribution in areas where land has been reused for farming and monuments destroyed.

Interest in rock art, once almost the exclusive concern of non-professional archaeologists, has greatly increased. It is recognised as such an important part of our history, as the earliest known form of communication in Northumberland, that serious measures are being taken to find out what threats there are to its preservation and how to present it to the public. The same applies to the preservation of archive material, such as my own – a relief to know that it will be well preserved and available to all. The most recent positive step has been the setting up of a Countryside Stewardship Scheme at the Chatton Park Hill sites at the request of the farmer, Duncan Ord in 2002.

One of the most important ways forward in the study of rock art is to find sites that may be able to answer important questions, especially about dating. Despite the increase in the database we are still in the dark about many things, and may continue to remain like that. Archaeology may never be able to answer all our questions.

118–21 *Four decorated rocks:*
Millstone Burn and Horton (outcrops),
Weetwood wall, Weetwood cairn

7

CEREMONIAL MONUMENTS

The Neolithic period throughout Britain witnessed the construction of various forms of ceremonial monuments, including 'henges' and stone circles.

Henges and pits

The Wooler area has a large number of henges. A henge is an area enclosed by a circular ditch with an outside bank, making it useless as a defensive site, with one or two gaps for entrances. Before the recent discoveries of henges in the Wooler area, these types of monuments were already well known in Britain, especially the early Stonehenge, from which the term derives. (Strictly speaking, Stonehenge is not now a henge because it has an external ditch!) They come in many different shapes and sizes, and generally do not have evidence of domestic activity inside them. Most in Northumberland are from c.2400-2000 BC. Aerial photography in particular has been responsible for finding many. They were in existence in Neolithic times and continued in use into the early Bronze Age. At times it is difficult to distinguish them from other circular monuments. In Scotland and on the Milfield Plain their purpose may be complex: perhaps as open-air meeting places or as burial places. Many have timber posts inside them, giving them a strong ritual flavour. The largest, however, and oldest at Coupland may have been a centre for rounding up animals. Again, we must learn not to think of domestic, everyday functions as separate from 'religion'. Circular enclosures suggest that what happened in the centre was for powerful, privileged people, those 'in the know', while the rest waited outside.

The Milfield henges are spaced out over intervals of 1-2km in an area 6km from north to south. Structurally they have little or nothing inside them apart from post pits and occasional rings of posts and later burials of the Anglo-Saxon period. The henges, varying in size and in orientation, were constructed by piling material dug from a circular ditch into an enclosing surrounding bank. Some were used for burial; some had uprights of stone or timber.

122 *West Akeld Steads: a henge and other crop marks.* NUM

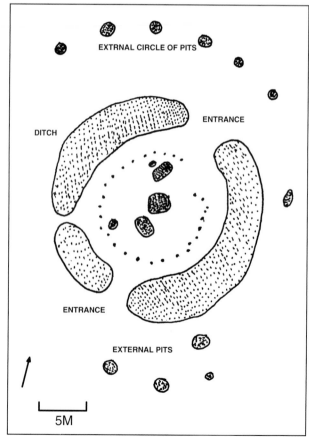

EXTRNAL CIRCLE OF PITS

DITCH

ENTRANCE

ENTRANCE

EXTERNAL PITS

5M

123 *North Milfield henge.* Based on A. Harding

Based on the ground plan of an excavated site, a henge has been reconstructed, with the experimental use of non-metal tools, at Milfield, where it is part of the Maelmin trail, the name attributed to an unexcavated seventh-century AD wooden palace of King Edwin nearby.

The Milfield North Henge (NT 939 335), which lies buried to the north of the reconstructed site, was excavated during a campaign of excavations led by Professor Anthony Harding (1981), who also drew attention to alignments of pits that 'may form large enclosures of ritual function' on the plain. At Thirlings (NT 956 322) Neolithic material came from pits and post pits. In one pit alone there were over 400 sherds representing a minimum of twelve pottery vessels, mainly bowls of different sizes. One had fingernail impressions with circular impressions below. Associated with the pottery was hazel, oak and birch charcoal. The same type of pottery was found in a post pit close by. In other pits some pottery with scored and twisted cord decoration was pressed into their clay lining. Bowls and straight-sided pots were associated with hazelnut shells. Another pit with similar pottery contained a sandstone saddle quern.

The North Henge (NT 934 348), with added Anglo-Saxon graves, had a roughly circular ditch, 4-5m across and 1.2-1.3m deep that was broad, flat-bottomed with sloping sides. It enclosed 30 small pits in a rough circle, with no certain traces that they were made to take posts, although it is generally assumed that they did. Inside this circle was a cist without filling or traces of a body. Other pits were probably graves; one had fragments of pottery and stone packing, another had a flint scraper and a third had an almost complete pot with, perhaps, a wooden coffin. Another oblong pit may also have been a grave. Outside the henge were pits arranged in a circle. Of those excavated, one contained six barbed and tanged arrowheads of the early Bronze Age period. There was little trace of a bank, which may have been ploughed flat.

The Milfield South Henge (NT 939 335) was excavated in 1977/8, exposing a large part of the interior and ditch, which proved to have been built in segments and flat-bottomed with a single entrance. The focal point of the interior was a deep pit in the west-central part that appeared as a dark patch 3.6 x 3.2m which proved to have been dug originally with a rectangular stone setting at its base. Burnt material that included a cup-marked stone was placed in the pit in the early Bronze Age, then a large post was inserted, not to the pit bottom, and big stones used to pack it. The post was later removed and the pit slumped in. There is no evidence that the pit was for a burial. There is a possible link here with what was found at the Blawearie cairn, centred on a large pit that bore no traces of burial (see above).

Other henge sites have subsequently been investigated. The most recent excavation, by Dr Clive Waddington (1997) at Coupland, became nationally known because the earliest carbon dates made it older than Stonehenge. Its function is likely to have been as a cattle enclosure, with tracks leading into it and through it from the surrounding hills, including a partial hollow way from

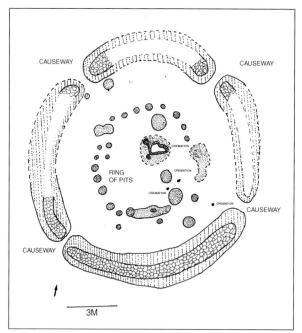

124 *Whitton: east of Milfield.* Based on R. Miket

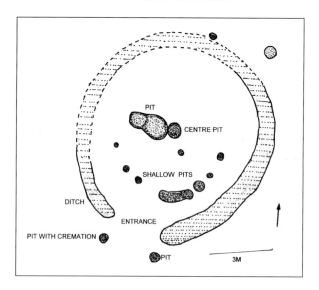

125 *Whitton: east of Milfield and the A697.* Based on R. Miket

the rich prehistoric site of Roughting Linn, which has the largest rock art panel in northern England and a large curved enclosure of many ditches and banks.

Roger Miket (1976; 1985) has done considerable work in the area, notably his excavation of the Neolithic site at Thirlings and the excavation of two burial areas just north of Milfield village; I was fortunate to be able to help on one site. There is a cluster of at least eleven ring-ditches in this area centred on NT 933 347. One excavated site lying to the east of the A697 out of Milfield village had a V-shaped ditch 2m wide and 1.2m deep with four causeways (i.e.

gaps into the centre through the ditch). Whinstone and sandstone blocks were set along the centre of the ditch (a very unusual feature) covered with burnt material containing burnt bone, wood, hazelnuts and pottery. There was an internal ring of pits and a larger pit at the centre with cremation, and three others with cremations. The plan of this site is very like that of the henges, and the dates are close. The stone packing in the ditch makes it different from other sites, and the excavator found evidence that it had slanting rafters coming from this wall to meet uprights in the inner circle. Its four access points are different too from henges. The burials took place before the construction of the building over them.

To the west of the A697, on sloping ground almost opposite the monument just described, is another excavated site, West Whitton. A U-shaped ditch with a narrow bank of sand and gravel just beyond its outer lip enclosed twelve very shallow pits, some with small whinstone boulders in them. A centre pit was steep-sided, flat-bottomed, containing at least 23 poorly-cremated individuals, sealed by a sandstone flag. West of it was a pit with sandstone and whinstone fragments, three angular upright stones and sandy earth with bone fragments. There was a shallow pit north of the ditch and two pits flanking the southern entrance.

There remain many unexcavated sites in this area; an aerial photograph that I took shows a henge picked out in the grass of Wooler cricket ground. Here we see not only the survival under the grass of a simple henge, but also of rig and furrow ploughing, probably of medieval date.

126 *Wooler cricket ground: a henge and rig and furrow*

Stone circles

There is a remarkable contrast between Cumbria and Northumberland in that the latter has few stone circles, those remaining being rather low-key affairs. Visits to Long Meg, Castlerigg and Swinside in Cumbria, for example, leave us with a sense of awe and wonder. The purpose of stone circles, despite very careful recording throughout Britain, has not been fully explained, either because there has been little excavation or because they were likely to be used for different purposes. I think of them as important community centres; bearing in mind that farms must have been scattered, there may have been a need for people to meet periodically at fixed points. So we have the equivalent of a market, a place for a chat, a religious centre where the tribe's identity was reinforced and their territory claimed. Unless there has been an extensive removal of other stone circles (and this is possible, considering the number that we know used to exist), some other centres must have served the same purpose in non-stone circle areas. Henges could have been a good substitute, and some combined ditch and wall with standing stones. Many stone circles have incorporated earlier timber circles, and we know that timber circles stood within some of Northumberland's henges.

One of the largest of Northumberland's circles is at Hethpool (NT 892 278), on the floor of the College Valley, on the slopes of which are numerous settlements and dramatic field systems. The circle is a rough horseshoe shape, 16 x 42.7m, with only eight stones remaining, together with some possible outliers.

Threestoneburn, Ilderton (NT 971 205) is a stone circle also sited in the Cheviots. Its granite stones formed a flattened circle 36 x 29m in a beautifully atmospheric part of the Cheviot Hills. The tallest stone is 1.7m and the smallest 53cm.

There are a few small circles, of which these are examples. Two of them, a circle at Duddo (NT 931 437) and a 'four poster' at Goatstones (NY 829 747)

127 *Duddo stone circle: a cremation burial site at the centre*

128 *Goatstones: a four-poster, with cup marks*

surround burials, their main function perhaps to draw attention to these burials. Another 'four poster', named The Three Kings because one of its stones had been toppled and was invisible, was also likely to have been built primarily to mark a burial (Burl, 1972). A circle at Nunwick Park, Simonburn, (NY 885 7410) is reported to have five stones, 2.4m high. Four stones of a plain ring 12.2m diameter are at Dod Law (NU 012 317).

Some words of caution: I have often been contacted about a stone circle near Haltwhistle not marked on the OS map. The reason is that a farmer decided he would like to build one for himself. The caution also applies to the erection of standing stones used by cattle to scratch themselves. These stones tend to be freshly quarried.

Standing stones

There are many standing stones scattered over the moorlands, some of them uninvestigated. The most famous are cup-marked stones at Matfen (NZ 032 705), The Warrior Stone at Ingoe (NZ 044 747), and the tallest at Swinburne (NY 939 746). All are in cultivated areas.

There are some massive 'standing stones' that may be natural, and many more smaller ones. It is not easy to tell whether they have been erected artificially unless their bases have been excavated. Some have probably rolled off hillsides, or have been carried by ice and dumped. When the strike of the sandstone rocks is vertical, weathering begins to flute the rock. In the Wooler area three large standing stones have been used since their erection to commemorate later events. These are The King's Stone near Flodden and the Battle Stones at Humbleton and Yeavering.

There is scope for much research into all these standing stones. Thorough searches, accurate recording and selective excavation will point the way forward to understanding them better, although the full reasons for their erection will remain a mystery.

Near to Holystone in the upper Coquet Valley there is a line of standing stones known as The Five Kings. In 1903 only four were standing, watched over by large cairns, the fifth having been 'removed to make a gatepost'. Dippie Dixon (1903) drew the remaining line from east to west, and Canon Greenwell commented that they were either part of a stone circle or part of an avenue.

There has been a great interest in the position of standing stones in relationship to astronomy, and alignments have been sought out. It has been suggested that Stonehenge functioned as some sort of astronomical computer, for example. The problem with speculating on alignments is that one can align anything with anything. When a stone is made to stand up, it is very

129-30 *Matfen and Swinburne cup marked standing stones*

131 *Sketch of the Five Kings in 1903.* D. Dixon

impressive. Why this has been done is not always understood, and the void is filled with many theories. On the one hand there is the reasonable assumption that in an agricultural community, observation of the heavens was important, as was the construction of some sort of calendar for the agricultural cycle would have been valuable. Sun is essential to life. Recumbent stone circles in north-west Scotland may well reflect the moon cycle. But we have to be careful in this business of alignments; it is easy to draw straight lines across a map that make it appear that some telephone boxes, some churches or some prehistoric sites are aligned, but so what?

Meanwhile, for those of us who do not wish to tangle with a plethora of unproved theories, the stones are there to be enjoyed for their own sake within the landscape. They have a life of their own, a language of their own that is personal to us.

There are some standing stones incorporated in cairns. At Lordenshaw there is a cairn standing on a cup marked outcrop at a prominent view point which has a small fluted standing stone at its centre at a place disturbed by barrow-diggers. Many cairns use standing stones as their kerbs, notably those at Blawearie and Chatton Sandyford, already described. The Blawearie stones are of all shapes and sizes, some fluted, erected in groups, whereas the Chatton Sandyford kerbs are more uniform and carefully tooled to produce a tight fit. The kerbed cairn echoes the stone circle, but its centre is filled in. At Temple Wood, Argyll, a large stone circle was closed off by the addition of horizontal slabs between uprights, and the centre then used to construct stone-covered cists, a change of function that took place over hundreds of years.

132 *Lordenshaw cairn built on decorated outcrop, incorporating a standing stone at the centre*

There is one other factor to take into account when we are considering monuments in the landscape. Paul Frodsham (Frodsham 1999; 2000) has drawn attention to the possible role of Iron Age hillforts as monuments, for he believes that they contain ceremonial architecture. They are not simply functional settlements. He observes that because the entrance to the fort of Yeavering Bell is facing due south, it is pointing to the distinctive profile of Hedgehope Hill. The construction of hillforts on the sites of early burial mounds could be to 'contain' them. At Chatton Park Hill the hillfort encloses a panel of outcrop prehistoric rock art that must have been obvious to the builders of the ramparts and ditches.

This comes back to the point made earlier in an examination of hillforts (chapter 4) that it is unlikely that hillforts were just there in a defensive role, but as possible markers, meeting places for scattered communities, animal enclosures and ritual centres. At the Ringses hillfort on north Beanley Moor, the use of the enclosure as a defence is negated by the fact that the ditches would give cover to attackers! Perhaps in the late Bronze Age and Iron Age some of the functions of the stone circles and henges had been taken over by the hillforts.

8

FRAGMENTS OF LIVES

Stone artefacts and tools

We still value some stones for their rarity and beauty; in prehistory the stones most highly valued were amber and jet. However, it is flint, chert and quartz that were essential to a way of life before the discovery of metals; traditions of working them lasted for thousands of years. Some regions of Britain were better placed than others for finding and using high quality flint. At first it was picked off the surface, but it was later mined. The finest quality material was not only admired for its usefulness as an artefact that reflected the skill of the craftsman, but also for its intrinsic beauty and rarity. Northumberland does not have the best sources of flint, so some of it had to be retrieved from glacial deposits, gravel and shingle, and other flints came from some distance away (for example from Yorkshire). It was therefore used carefully to conserve stocks. Perhaps there was a rate of exchange for it.

Some people have assumed that because there is flint on the coast, that some of this could have been used. However, some of it may have been brought in by recent sea trade to act as ballast in ships returning to Northumberland ports.

When I am showing children the value of flint as a tool, I produce a large nodule or slab of it, wrap it in a heavy cloth and smash it with a hammer. We then examine the results. Bearing in mind that the users would be looking for arrow points, knives, and scrapers, it is not difficult to see that, even without further work, flint is an ideal material. An examination of tools made in prehistoric times shows that in order to make the required shapes, some further work was needed. Pressure, for example, with bone or antler, will flake small pieces of flint to make a sharp, shaped edge. Looking rather like toffee, flint breaks up according to how it is struck. A common feature is a 'bulb of percussion' that looks like a small swelling. The core itself, from which blades have been struck, could be fashioned into a tool.

In a non-flint area, the presence of worked flint and flakes on the surface when a field has been ploughed is the surest indication of prehistoric people. The odd arrowhead may have been lost by a hunter, but a concentration of

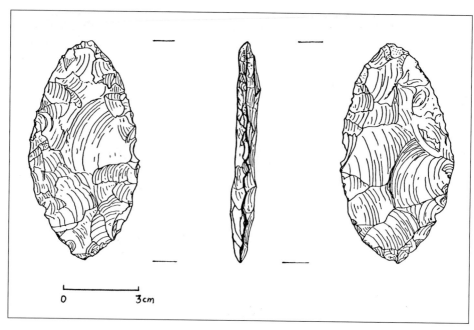

133 *The art of the flint knapper: a discoidal flint knife found by F. Berthele at Wark-on-Tweed.*
Drawn by Mary Hurrell (NUM)

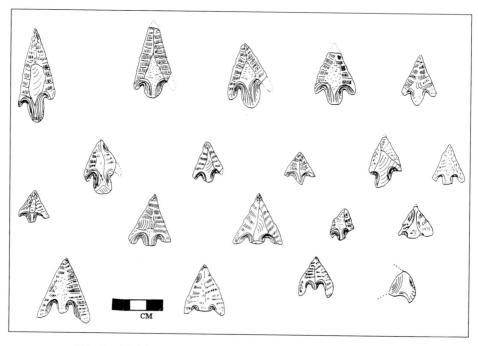

134 *Late Neolithic/Early Bronze Age arrowheads from F. Berthele's collection*

135 *The Berthele collection includes polished axes, maceheads, battle axes, and rubbing stones (some of the latter are probably not prehistoric)*

flakes shows that people stopped for a while or lived there when they made the tools of their trade. These tools changed slowly in form over time, and this enables us to identify particular prehistoric people by association with other things found in the field. Thus Mesolithic people, the earliest that we find evidence for in Northumberland, made thin long blades known as microliths to barb and tip their arrows. Broader flakes became used as scrapers, knives and arrowheads. Saws were also made, as flint can be serrated with small notches.

Some tools used for killing, cutting and scraping display only slight variations over thousands of years, but we can identify some that were made in the Neolithic and others in the early Bronze Age. For example, leaf-shaped arrowheads are earlier than those with barbs and tangs. Discoidal polished knives and plano-convex knives are associated with the late Neolithic/early Bronze Age. Once a site or group of flints can be associated with a particular people and time, any subsequent discovery of such artefacts can then be 'dated'. The more you find, the more you become competent at recognising this.

The illustrations show some of the range of artefacts.

Axes

Stone was valued for the axes that could be made from it. Special rock, such as Langdale stone from the Lake District, was so prized that over 2,000 axes made there have been found all over Britain and Ireland. Those from Northumberland are part of that trade, dating from about 5,500 years ago. There are 33 other known distinct sources of 'special' stone from Britain.

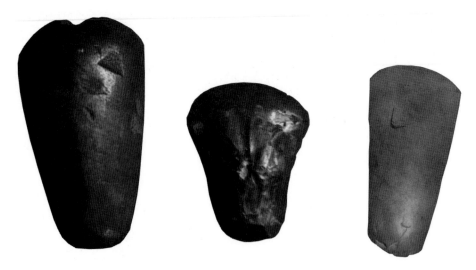

136-7 *Polished stone axes from Felton (ACM) and a Langdale axe from Milfield*

However, flint was the most important raw material. Axes were needed for the forest and scrub clearance that was the beginning of farming, and as wood-working tools, although some were more useful as ornaments than tools. There is one particular axe from Lilburn that is made of flint, but has an expanding cutting edge that is like a copper axe; this suggests that the maker was imitating a newly-introduced metal style in stone.

A modern example

The late Bob Robson, a roadman from Swarland, near Felton, whose interest in prehistory was based on observation and practicality, made a polished axe from a piece of whinstone (dolerite), 'partly fashioned by nature', that he had found near Warkworth bridge. It took him about 52 hours to complete it. His record lists each day that he worked, how long he spent, and what methods he used. He started by holding it in a vice, hitting it with a chisel, but made little progress because it was much harder than flint. He 'chipped, chopped and filed', sometimes holding it under the tap, and spent hours rubbing it. During the process his son (also called Bob and an amateur archaeologist) declared that it looked OK. Bob wrote that towards the end of his project 'the carborundum was wearing thin'. He had started on 24 July 1967, was working on the night of 15 August until midnight and finished with the words 'I've made it!' at 1.30am on 16 August. He also devised a method of hafting it. This has been donated to the Museum of Antiquities, Newcastle. Its only fault is a small piece chipped off the cutting edge; perhaps someone with less respect for the man-hours spent on it had used it on something other than wood.

138 *Bob Robson's homemade polished whinstone axe. It took 52 hours to complete*

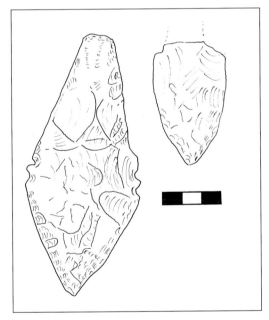

139 *A flint knife, prepared for hafting, from Tarset (NY 739 9120), and a volcanic one from Kielder (NY 632 924); scale cm*

Cutting tools

In addition to polished and unpolished knives, there are slightly curved sickles and razors. They are for working leather, meat, wood and fibres. There are large wide blades that are re-touched. Some have a silica gloss left on the surface after years of cutting vegetation. Small finely-worked knives are characteristic of the later Neolithic and early Bronze Age.

Pointed tools are used for boring holes in wood and other material, opening shells, and drilling holes in bone; these can be made by working flint blades into sharp, narrow points.

Scrapers

Everyone needed to peg out animal skins, scrape out the inside to clean them, and then form them into clothes and shelter. After worked blades, the scrapers used for this are the most common of all on Neolithic sites. They vary from thumb-sized to fist-sized. They can be retouched along one or more edges. The simplest are 'side' scrapers.

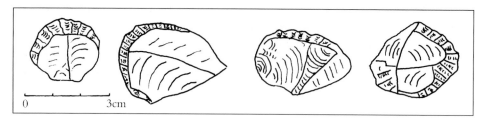

0   3cm

140 *Four typical scrapers for cutting and scraping skins*

141 *A 'battle axe' from Linkey Law, Chatton with its distinct hour-glass drilled perforation*

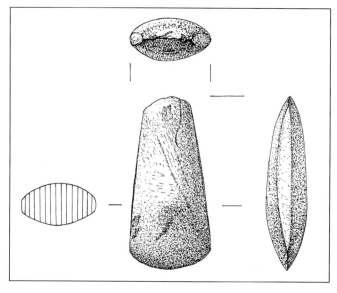

142 *A Cumbrian polished stone axe from Langdale, found by a schoolboy on the Milfield Plain.* Drawing by Mary Hurrell (NUM)

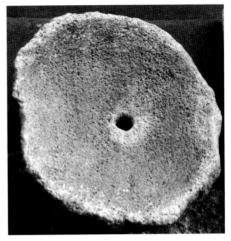

143 *An unusual granite rotary quern from the Cockshaw Burn, Hexham*

Other stone objects

These include hammers, maces, and perforated battle-axes belonging to the late Neolithic and are well represented in our museums. It required skill to bore the hole. Maces are status symbols. Stone balls from Scotland may have a similar symbolism.

Polishers, which may be smooth, flat or rounded stones are used on hides. Other stones are used to grind corn, the simplest being saddle querns of the type still known in Third World communities, where a rubbing stone is used on a curving stone platform to grind corn. These querns develop in sophistication over time, as we see in the illustration, for a handle was added to turn two stones that rubbed against each other.

All this information comes from many sources. The most common is from walking a field after it has been ploughed, either systematically on a grid pattern or randomly. One of the largest and most important collections was made by 'Fritz' Berthele, who in his work with forestry was able to look at land ploughed prior to tree-planting, and which may not be available for inspection for many decades (see chapter 3). The collection, now in private hands in Chillingham castle, has taken an incalculable time to amass (Hewitt 1995). I walked with Fritz one day for hours, and we found only one flint. A field may yield very little until ploughing turns the soil sufficiently to reveal its artefacts. Many other finds have been made, and many have fortunately been recorded, for where they are found is as important as what is found. An important collection of flints and fragments of jewellery from the Blawearie area of Old Bewick Moor was found by the Rogerson family, who were shepherds there (Newbigin 1936).

The picture becomes clearer when a site is excavated, for then the artefacts are in a context both vertically and horizontally. Interest in the contents of cairns has led to associated objects being found, such as the burnt scrapers in the cist burial of an adult and child at Blawearie. The burial of artefacts is an intriguing practice, for we cannot be sure exactly what the intention was.

Pottery

Just as agriculture revolutionised civilization, so the discovery of pottery-making heralded an industrial revolution. This seems to be a big claim for what often appears in some reports as page after page of drawings of potsherds, but its shaping, texture, firing and decoration are of vital importance in the archaeological record. In the absence of writing, the choice of patterns and images to decorate clay is an important aesthetic one. The fact that, like British rock art, the choice excluded animal and human forms, concentrating on symbols and motifs, gives it a distinctive quality. The process of manufacture and decoration went on for hundreds of years, with the greatest flowering of the art (to our eyes) taking place in the early Bronze Age. Pottery, mainly in the form of containers, was made both for domestic and funerary use. In the latter case, this implies that it was highly valued, as much as ornaments or weapons and tools, which it sometimes accompanies. However, this value did not extend evenly throughout the prehistoric period.

As a key to periods in prehistory, pottery is enormously valuable. Radiocarbon dating methods, acting as a check, have made it more reliable. As different regions produced variations on fairly standard themes of manufacture and design, as in rock art – where the basic symbols were manipulated to get different individual results – we can begin to see regions with their own dec-

144 *Beakers from Lesbury, Beanley and Amble in Alnwick Castle Museum*

145 *Bolton House Food Vessel: one of the most attractive and ornate.* ACM

orations. By examining the clay structure, the sources of raw material may be defined. If some pottery is traded, it may be traced to its source. Luckily, pottery survives well, unlike organic material. It is even possible to establish that some patterns were created with the help of materials such as twisted cord or bones; in rare cases grain becomes mixed up with the clay before it is baked, and it is possible to identify the type and to obtain C14 dates from the grains.

Wheel-turned pottery was not made until the late Iron Age, so the earlier types were the result of making it from slabs and coils of clay. It is not difficult to make, and practice can lead to good results. As in every society, there will be individuals who become particularly good at it. But what is pottery for? Names that have been given to particular styles of pottery, such as Beaker and Food Vessel, and are still used, but when the terms were first coined by archaeologists the assumption was that one contained liquid, the other food, for the next world. This was the result of most pottery being found in burials. Then people became aware that some pottery could be used both in burials and domestic settlements. In the late Bronze Age, pots used in everyday life were indistinguishable from those buried with the dead, and this coincided with a lack of interest in building more burial mounds. Instead, old ones were reused. Had the symbolic value of pottery changed?

There are good clays all over Britain. Clay was mixed with fillers (e.g. crushed burnt flint, shell, straw). Pots were made in all shapes and sizes; at different times they were flat-bottomed, round-bottomed, some had impressed bands, an overall pattern, no pattern, a decorated top of rim, lugs, handles, knobs, cordons. They were fired in bonfires or pit kilns. Pots were used for storage and cooking, but their designs indicate a regional identity. This is obvious in a burial context, but pottery can also be buried significantly in other

146 *Early prehistoric round-bottomed pot from Thirlings excavations*

contexts such as pits; there can appear to be some sort of logic to its position in settlements and ritual places, where pottery was more than just a utilitarian thing. Its burial at certain places gave it a significance that is difficult for us to understand, partly because we so often keep usefulness and symbolism apart.

To modern eyes some prehistoric pottery is very attractive, because the shape and decoration appeal. The makers must have made it as an ornament, not just some useful thing. They probably experimented with all kinds of objects to mark the clay surface, discovering what children discover when they are put in the same situation: that combs, wheels, points, sharp edges, cut straws, feathers, thumb pressure and nails produce impressions. Clay can be squeezed into ridges; extra pieces can be stuck on. Then it is a case of repeating an effect to produce a pleasant pattern.

There is much pottery available in our archaeological record. Its position in some places is already noted in this book, so I shall give a few examples of different types from different periods as a general guide. Changes can be hard to explain, but the recognition of pottery typologies is an important tool for the archaeologist. There are plenty of examples on show in local museums.

1. Early Neolithic

The earliest is known generally now as early (or 'earlier') Neolithic, ranging from 4000-3000 BC; a very long tradition! It was, and still is in some publications, known as Grimston-Lyles Hill pottery, after sites in Yorkshire and Antrim. It has a wide distribution in Britain and hundreds of years earlier on the continent, suggesting that when it came into use here it was already a well-developed tradition. It has a rounded base, fairly plain and shallow. It sometimes has shoulders ('carinated') with lugs. There are many varieties that are being increasingly found in Scotland, with more ornate decoration than the usual. In Northumberland one of the best sources of early pottery is the Milfield Plain and Ford. Decoration is simple, using circular and lined incisions, most frequently confined to the top of the vessels. As it develops, it becomes more elaborate in decoration and is given the term Impressed Ware (or Peterborough Ware); the bowls are thick-rimmed, round based, and heavily decorated with reeds, sticks, small bones and whipped cord. It was fully developed by 3000 BC, and some of the styles of decoration continued for many more hundreds of years.

2. Grooved Ware

The next recognisable phase is Grooved Ware (formerly called Rinyo-Clacton), strongly associated with later Neolithic ritual sites in the south and with northern settlements. There are bucket-, tub- and barrel-shaped vessels, flat-based, with heavy grooves, ribs and cordons. In Scotland this pottery can have chevrons cut into the clay, dotted cordons and lozenge shapes. In Ireland this pottery appears significantly in the chambered tombs of the Boyne valley.

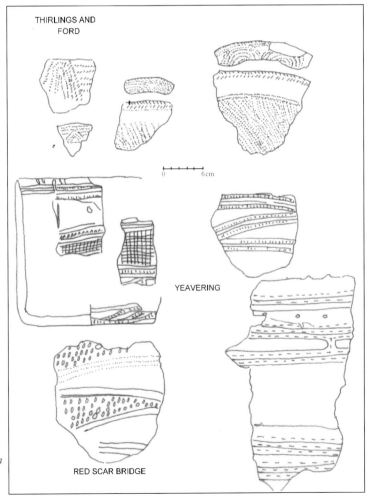

THIRLINGS AND FORD

0   6 cm

YEAVERING

RED SCAR BRIDGE

147 *Early pottery from the Milfield Plain and Yeavering.* Berwick Museum

151

148 *Pottery of different early Bronze Age types, with bone and cremated bone.* ACM

3. Beaker period

The final Neolithic and early Bronze Age period has more decorative pots. Trade links with Europe brought in more styles. Beakers are a major European pottery tradition and played an important part in burial, along with jewellery and tools. The Beaker appears *c.*2400 BC, a gentle S-shaped profile, decorated all over with incised lines, cord and comb patterns in horizontal lines. The middle Beaker period produced more decorative pottery, with diamonds, triangles, fingernail impressions, and cords. The neck became shorter, wider, and more curved in profile. Later Beaker (2000-1700 BC) saw a considerable change in shape. The neck became straight, almost vertical above a short bulbous body. The neck and belly were zoned, with cord impressions, and zones filled with geometric motifs and zigzags. At the same time the Food Vessel and

149 *Food Vessel Urn at the moment of discovery from Turf Knowe cairn north*

Urn styles developed with a small, flat-based bipartite, heavy rim; there were knobs, handles, cordons, and incisions. Collared urns appear at the same time. Eventually the Encrusted Urn made its appearance, with a heavy collared rim. These pottery forms take us through the Bronze Age, and are particularly used for cremation burials. We can see a considerable overlap in styles. The illustrations show what varieties there are.

Food Vessels and Collared Urns are still found in 1200 BC (Gibson 2002). Cordoned Urns are found only in Ireland, Scotland, the west and north of England. This great variety of pottery reaches its best in the early Bronze Age, but after that there is a decline. Why this should be is difficult to understand, even for those who make pottery a special study.

4. Post-1000 BC

After *c.*1000 BC in northern Britain we find mostly coarse buckets. Alex Gibson says this (2002): 'It is not possible to create a relative chronology for the Iron Age in the north of England and mainland Scotland based on ceramics.' The emphasis has been on southern England where there is lots of well-decorated pottery, with regional variations. It contrasts with the coarse northern ware, looking back to Bronze Age bowls and urns. There is currently no means of dating sites from such pottery. Despite all the northern hillforts with their implied regional power focus, there is no real evidence of any rich culture. It never came under continental influence as the ancient 'Golden Triangle' of the south-east did, and after the Roman conquest the area north of Hadrian's Wall remained a backwater, at least in its pottery. It did without the mass-produced pottery that flooded the English markets to the south.

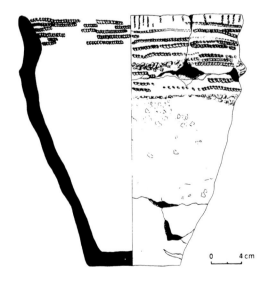

0   4 cm

150 *Blawearie excavation: the last deposit was this Food Vessel Urn with two cremations*

Metalwork

For thousands of years stone was the main source of tools and weapons. The discovery of metals did not at once displace stone; the techniques of extracting metal from ore, smelting, re-heating, moulding, or using other means of shaping metal became more sophisticated with use, confined to fewer craftsmen, and production and exchange were perhaps controlled by a few powerful people.

At first copper was used on its own, and ended up along with Beaker pottery in select graves. This does not mean that there was an invasion and conquest by a cultured elite, but a sharing in a widespread admiration for what new technology was providing elsewhere. This technology could only have crossed the Channel, but then its adoption would have spread. Articles found in graves of this early period show no signs of wear, and seem intended as ornaments. As technology developed with the addition of other minerals to copper, such as tin, to make bronze, the continuing use of metals in graves suggests that it was valued as a sign of the owner's power. Much of our knowledge of prehistoric metalwork, up to the later Iron Age, comes largely from burials and from hoards. These hoards may be in some cases an unclaimed cache buried for safety by some metal-founder, or ritually buried as an offering to the gods. Deposits in burials, in water, in select places in the landscape and settlements can only be seen as part of a belief system the details of which elude us.

Once the desired metal objects arrived from the continent, local prominent people who wanted to own more could have employed skilled workers and innovators to develop local sources. The most basic form was the axe. Stone axes had existed for thousands of years and reached a state of almost-perfection in specialised manufacturing centres such as the Lake District, where andesite tuff had a beauty and mystique that led to it being exported all over Britain and Ireland. The photograph of a flint axe found in a field in the Lilburn area (its exact location is not known), part of the Berthele collection, is a very interesting example of the transition from high quality stone to metal. Made of flint, this axe has an expanding edge, a characteristic of early copper axes. Compare this with the copper axe from Corbridge and it can be seen where the idea for the shape came from; there is a difference, though, in the decoration that the craftsman was able to apply to the metal. There are plenty of examples of what decorative symbols and motifs could be used, similar to those used on Beaker pottery.

To stay with the axe for a while, its development continues for hundreds of years, and its development makes it possible to date these axes. One can imagine the impact of the first sight of the first copper axe to arrive in the region. Here people would have used stone axes as part of everyday life, and the arrival of a shiny axe made of an unknown material might have appeared magical. The people who could produce these things from the ground, so to speak, must have been regarded with awe. Apart from wanting one, people would have wanted to know how they could make them for themselves. This was revolutionary.

151 (Opposite) *Axe and spear moulds in Alnwick Castle Museum*

152-3 *A decorated copper flat axe from Corbridge (right) and a polished flint axe from Lilburn imitating the expanding edge (above).* ACM; Berthele collection

154 *A bronze shield in Newcastle Museum of Antiquities*

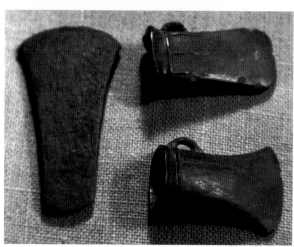

155 *From flat axe to socketed and looped varieties.* ACM

The shape and form of axes is determined by the qualities of the metal they were made from, by the nature of the moulds, and by the chosen methods of hafting them. To fly off the handle would have been a serious matter. An examination of the development of the copper and bronze axe shows how 'palstaves' (flat axes) had a flared blade and distinct shoulders, often with the addition of a stop-ridge to hold the wooden shaft in place.

Socketed axes had a central hollow to secure the haft, and 'looped' palstaves made use of an additional leather thong for the same purpose. Some are so small that they may well have been woodworking tools rather than weapons, but when we turn to knives, rapiers, swords and spears there is hardly a peaceful intention there: they were to be used for hacking and stabbing. Metal

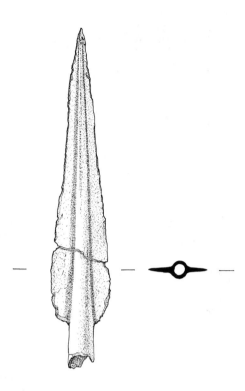

156 *A Bronze Age spearhead from Alnwick.*
Drawn by Mary Hurrell

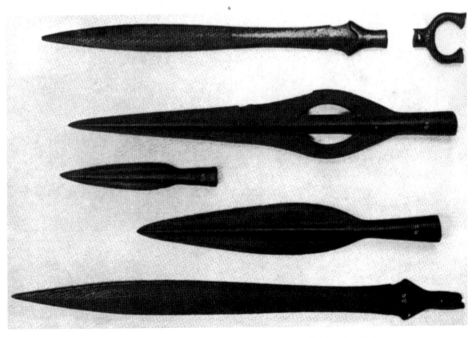

157 *The Whittingham hoard. County History* 1935 vol. XIV

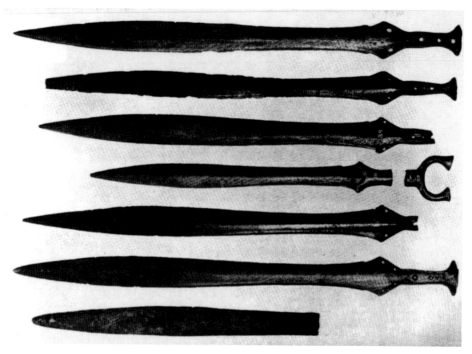

158 *Swords from top: Amersidelaw, Brandon, Whittingham, Whittingham, Ewart, Ewart and South Lyham. CH XIV*

159 *Spear heads from Farnley and Corbridge. ACM*

shields could have been used only for ceremonies, but their existence presupposes hand–to–hand warfare.

What has always puzzled me is *why* people decided to take such valuable items out of circulation by burying them; 'ritual' considerations may cover this, but I don't know how.

I have chosen to give pictorial examples to show variety and development in metal objects. Further details are referenced in the Bibliography, particularly Burgess (1968, 2002).

9

SYMBOLS OF POWER

Some people express their status in life by displaying objects that are often non-utilitarian, exotic, expensive and exclusive. 'What do you give to people who have everything?' is something that we might hear today. The answer: something new that they do not already have or a more unusual/expensive/rare version of what they already have. Power may express itself as a graduation from a Mini to a Rolls Royce, a tie of an exclusive club, membership of a secret order, or even the acquisition of a rare painting or ornament. The value of the object is that it proclaims status – the outward and visible sign (often without the inward spiritual grace!) of what some people accept as success. The size of one's possessions, the quality of clothes and ornaments and offices showered upon them are familiar enough signs.

The story of the Widow's Mite is a reminder that some people need to display even their giving. With a loud voice one proclaims himself not as other men are, and deposits his offering with a resounding clunk. The poor widow gives all she can afford quietly and unobtrusively. Having a surplus to distribute is a sign of power. It can be used to reinforce the hold of that power over others, who, if they make the right noises, may receive more bounty. Other people's sense of obligation is a weapon used by the powerful. The exercise of power, be it financial, spiritual or sexual, can also be cruel in its imposition of fear.

In 1985 an impressive exhibition was held at the National Museum of Antiquities of Scotland, Edinburgh, entitled 'Symbols of Power'. This was designed to concentrate on 'aspects of a single theme, the manifestation of power, prestige and status in the third and second millennia BC'. The book that accompanied the exhibition followed these headings: 'The use of the ancestors'; 'From ancestors to gods'; 'The acknowledgement of individual power'; and 'The importance of craftsmanship'. I shall try to gather these 'symbols' together and discuss how they relate to prehistoric Northumberland.

When people die, the memory of them or their mortal remains may be cherished for what they represent. Ancestors lay claims to the land; each one may have been revered by keeping others alive and enriching them. Their

160 *The Poind and his Man: a burial mound and standing stone with views to Simonside, at Shaftoe*

death may be marked by some ceremony. They may join other ancestors in a specific place, such as a tomb that strengthens a sense of belonging and contribution to the tribe. The more the tribe thinks of itself, the more grandiose the monument may become. The monument may then lay claim to the land and to the tradition of the people. Look, we are here! This is ours! This is what we have achieved!

This power, this sense of continuity and achievement, may not be solely attributable to people themselves, but to other forces working on their behalf. Supernatural intervention, the help of the 'gods', enriches early literature, but it may have been wished for, asked for, in ways not clear to us. Burial mounds and the practices that accompany them are visible and understandable expressions of value, but the presence of other monuments such as standing stones, circles of wood and stone and other engineered projects suggests that someone is drawing in force from the outside to a centre and, in the case of some of our largest monuments, reaching for the skies. Are gods being thanked, invoked, propitiated by such constructions? Do people continue to influence life through the gods after they are dead? Do people move on to another place, and if so, do they need anything to take with them? Do people want spirits to be around them, or would they rather that spirits stay away? Is the purpose of a capstone and mound over a burial pit a desire to keep the ancestors below ground?

It has often been said that one of the changes from the early Neolithic to late Neolithic/early Bronze Age burial practices was a movement away from the idea of a community of people being in one burial place to an emphasis on the individual. Round mounds were used for both practices at different times, with some of the most outstanding examples, with their rock art, being in the Boyne valley of Ireland. There was a move away from the chambered tomb under a mound to cist burials. What then happened to all the other people who were not given a formal burial? We don't know, it was probably left to the forces of nature. This means that those who were buried individually were regarded as special in some way. The appearance of Beakers, those delicate, well-proportioned and well-decorated vessels, in graves was a sign of the importance of the people that they accompanied. Fine stone implements accompany some, and jewellery of jet and amber; with the introduction of metals we have a new kind of status symbol that accompanies the dead. Some archaeologists see these rare metals, much more difficult to access than stone, as an even greater method of establishing the importance of the people who owned them, for there was a greater control over their production, known only to very few specialist smiths. If you can control the means of production, you wield great power.

To dispose of a precious artefact in a burial is also a demonstration of great power, either of the person who owned it or of the person who decided to take it out of circulation. One example was a gold basket-shaped 'earring' from a burial at Kirkhaugh. This object, at the Museum of Antiquities of Newcastle, was such a rare thing that one wonders what was going on there. We can only guess. It was found at the centre of a ring cairn, with disturbed Beaker, equal barbed and tanged arrowhead.

Objects of metal such as axes and chisels may not be used much in woodwork, few show signs of use when they are in burials, so they could have been valued more for status than practicality. This happened too with stone axes from Langdale, Cumbria; these are not just part of the workaday world.

Individuals too could control the rituals of power; they could have ordered the building of stone circles and other monuments and may have decided who was allowed in and who did what. If they also controlled food supply and provided feasts for people attending rituals, their power was great indeed. Yet power is not always imposed against people's wills. Communal buildings, be they tombs, circles or hillforts, demand the organisation of labour on a large scale, and this is best done by consent. External threats could reinforce the tribal identity. Seeking help from the gods through monuments was in everyone's interest.

There was a time when objects found in water, such as rivers, were thought to have been accidentally lost. Now it is clear that much of value was made as

161 *A polished axe imported from the popular Langdale quarries; more ornamental than useful, it would appear, as few show signs of wear*

162 *A bronze sword from Amersidelaw farm.* ACM

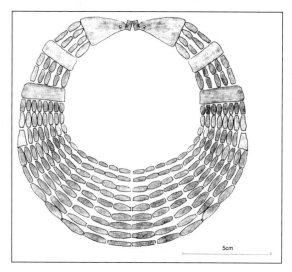

5cm

163 *Jet necklace from Kyloe.* Based on a reconstruction by T.G. Newman

a votive offering. Today a visit to an old castle with a well will often show how people still throw coins in. All hoards of metal, especially those buried, were thought to have been unclaimed, when in fact some were not meant to be dug up again. They were 'gifts to the gods'. But how can we tell the difference?

In Britain axes are the most common objects in these metal hoards, whereas daggers appear more with other objects such as beads in burials. If they are buried in a pit with no body, this must have been a conspicuous display of wealth and power, because the objects were given away to the earth. What did the donor assume was being given in return?

Objects that still appear attractive today include necklaces and beads. The amber necklace from Blawearie, although dulled by thousands of years in the ground, is a fine piece of work. This was not made, though, specifically for a burial, as it shows signs of long use, especially the pendant bead, the hole of which is almost worn through to the edge of the pendant, probably because it had been hanging around someone's neck by a string for so long.

The jet necklace found in a cist within the same mound, along with a broken flint knife, is made of narrow jet barrel beads interspersed with shale discs. The Kyloe necklace (Newman, 1976) is especially elaborate, and has parallels in other parts of Britain. These must be only a representative few. The Rogerson collection of objects from Old Bewick moor contains unprovenanced jet and shale beads and other objects (Newbigin, 1941). The land

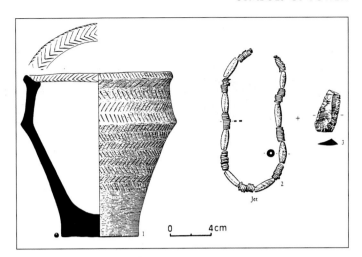

164 *Blawearie cairns Food Vessel, shale and jet necklace and flint knife from burials.* British Museum

165-6 (Above and right) *Jet and shale objects from moorland ploughsoil.* F. Berthele collection

ploughed for forest in the moorlands also produced similar objects, including a fine Iron Age bead, but we do not know precisely where they came from.

The blue 'melon' bead from the Blawearie cairn is later than the other objects in the cairn, and could have been inserted at any time from the Iron Age onwards. This indicates another kind of power: the power of an ancient site that needs to be acknowledged. My excavation of Money Mound in Sussex (Beckensall 1967) demonstrates a classic example of votive offerings. A massive Beaker burial cairn lying close to a hollow way that linked Roman

167 *Blawearie melon bead, a later votive insertion in the mound*

roads from London to the coast became the repository of pottery, beads and coins from the late Iron Age throughout the Roman occupation (over 200 coins). In another phase of history the disturbance of the same mound in the 1720s saw the centre of it scoured out in a search for treasure. That example covers intrusion at least two thousand years later than the mound.

What emerges from the study of well-crafted implements and ornaments is that the people who made them must have been highly regarded in the society that employed their talents. But what if they were slaves? Their work would still have been highly regarded, but the people who did the work may not. Where materials such as flint were essential to everyone's survival, tools were probably made by everyone; other materials such as metals were handled only by skilled craftsmen. Whether they formed a sort of Guild, an organisation of the elite who shared the secrets of their craft and withheld them from outsiders or worked individually under the protection and control of an overlord, we do not know.

Objects that show the power of their owners begin to take on a different form in the Bronze and Iron Ages, and we may detect in the emphasis on metal swords, spears and shields a use of these weapons, especially those made of iron, against people. Stone artefacts may be interpreted as part of a hunting, skinning economy that was always part of existence, although some of these were used in anger against people. The arrival of metal weapons coincided with the building of hillforts, and we see a division of land where territory is to be defended or as a springboard for conquest. People seemed to be getting nastier! With this apparent increased aggression came more concentration of power in the hands of a few, although Northumberland is not to the forefront with this kind of exhibitionism. Those areas closest to Europe adopted the new fashions, and although in Northumberland we have many sites that may cover this period, the level of material culture is lower. In a sense, those people in the south who experienced Continental trade were all prepared for the goodies that the invaders brought with them at the price of submission, voluntarily or through force. It took much longer to reach the outposts of empire later defined by the Roman Wall.

10

ENDPIECE

My interest in prehistoric archaeology began in Sussex when I agreed to give a talk on prehistoric Sussex to a WEA group whose lecturer was indisposed. I knew little about the subject, but had time to learn. Some of the class brought with them some of the finest flint implements that I have ever seen, and I was hooked.

My growing interest was reinforced when I signed up for an excavation on the South Downs, where some of my time was spent trowelling in a very large Iron Age gatepost hole in an unfinished hillfort. The company was skilled and learned. All were 'amateurs', which to me meant that they were there for the love of archaeology rather than as a job. I remember hearing my first archaeology joke there, something that I have repeated at lectures to new audiences.

It is about the quiz programme, 'Animal, Vegetable and Mineral' several hundred years from now, when experts are asked to identify and explain the function of some antique and enigmatic object. The arrival of a teapot drew various responses: it could have been a baby's feeding bottle or a musical instrument, but the 'Mortimer Wheeler' of the day declared that it was an object used in ritual, fertility cults. A priest carried the vessel to an altar. A second priest lifted the lid and placed a leaf inside the vessel. A third priest poured in boiling water. The expert leaned back, as though satisfied with his explanation. The question master asked what this had to do with fertility. 'Ah,' said the expert, 'someone then asks "Who's going to be mother?"' Brilliant!

I arrived in Northumberland in 1966 after two years in Malta. My road to Damascus led me to Old Bewick Moor where I came face to face with a mystery that has remained with me since and become the focus of much of my work: the large cup and ring marked rock set in a landscape rich in the past, evocative and powerful.

Part of my reaction to this landscape has been through poetry. In this, for example:

Rough moorland throbs against pale pasture,
Meets mosaics on stone walls:
A life beyond a life: one calm and smooth,
One rifted, broken up and full of mystery.
And at this meeting place
A tilted table rock, absorbing light,
Libating gold from man-made grooves;
Fluidity, concentric circles leaping into life
And fading with the sun-slip down the scarp.
Black rooks erupt above stiff Douglas fir,
Blown fragments from a fire
That drift awhile, and rest.
Like giant wings, the shadows of the night
Beat out the light.
Blawearie house absorbs a depth of red
That hovers the warm air
Before magenta in the sky cries welcome to the stars.

This book is the result of all kinds of experience, building on those early foundations of developing awareness of what riches landscapes have to offer. Interest in archaeology gives visits into the countryside a focus. Sometimes it reaches the parts that nothing else will touch; the lonely, isolated, remote areas experienced in all weathers, in all seasons. Places that are reassuring, that encourage a sense of belonging. Places that are uneasy, weird, and sometimes frightening. As a teacher I know that the best incentive for learning is interest; I learn most when I am excited, inspired. If archaeology does not generate an emotional response of some sort, it can be like an empty wineskin. Its essence is people and their lives, lived in a landscape that awaits interpretation and understanding.

We are constantly told that history is about people. That's hard to believe when we read some archaeological reports that seem to drain everything alive away – including our rich language. Yet 'people' of the past are very difficult to reach. This book has covered thousands of years of change, yet how can we see the 'people' who inhabited this land? Not a name to give to those who made pottery, dug ditches, looked after the cattle, helped to build burial cairns or hillforts. A skeleton or a pot full of cremated bones may be all that is left of a person. I cannot pretend to see 'people' from the past when nothing has been written down by them or their contemporaries to tell me about them. Yet I can still sense their presence in the landscape, in fragments they have left behind. I trust that we have feelings in common, hopes and fears.

Humbleton Hill overlooks the Milfield Plain from the edge of the volcanic Hills across the scarplands to the North Sea. I offer the reader a poem in which I try to convey the complexity of what I feel about places like this:

High Humbleton

High Humbleton, bare-headed hill, with half-closed eyes
Takes in pale shadow shapes
That flit across the valley's furrowed flatlands
Among flecked feeding gulls, scorning this idle game
Devised by sun and clouds.

A hillfort tonsure of grey rock tumbles to its neck
And bears indignity of hikers' cairn heaped on its head,
Shoulders hunched against the cold.
Its ancient body crinkles into unknown depths
From which he rose from molten rock,
Roaring defiance, blacking sun
Until the hissing chaos of his pent-up anger ceased.

Margin of ice-scoured, rounded, clustered hills
With tree-strewn cleughs
Focused on flat-topped Cheviot;
This hill an eastern sentinel.

Bracken's copper, laced with bright green winter grass
From summer's feet and narrow tread of sheep,
Spreads like a rash.
Heather, tight in clusters, raises dust
In raked mid-winter sun
To mark the passage of a badger or a fox.
There is a stillness that no life can shake,
No re-arrangement of the sun-tossed clouds
Can penetrate the surface of the hills.
Below the scanty soil are vesicles of blown-out gas
Replugged with shining minerals in rich red rock,
Forever hard and cold.

A lingering light upon cold hills and sunward slopes
Coaxes a story thousands of seasons long.
Barrows for the dead, like crusted pimples
Break the sloping ground,
And cord rig combs the hillside, once a bed of grain,
Scarcely a mouthful now for sullen sheep.
Faint hollow ways and intermittent walls
Grow and fade with moving light.

Shallow pits of shadows speak
Of houses in enclosures platform-perched
Or huddled round the hillfort's top.
These soils are wasted now.
Only deep-set lynchets or the massive hillfort walls stand proud.
Only a patient eye can now detect
The traces of the face beneath the veil,
And Humbleton has seen it all.
When moonrise mists the valleys with its eerie light
The dark mass broods and gathers to itself
So many lives, so many times.

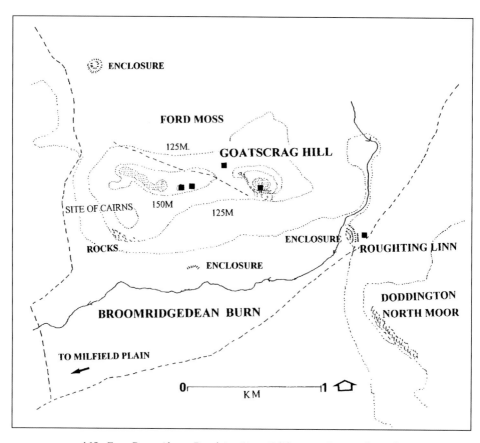

168 *From Broomridge to Roughting Linn. Solid squares denote rock panels*

PLACES TO VISIT

As Northumberland is a very large county with hundreds of prehistoric sites, I have concentrated on a small number that you might like to visit. These are determined by accessibility, and by what other joys the Northumberland landscape has to offer.

Care must be taken over access; where sites are not open to the public, permission is needed from the landowner.

I have divided the county into two general areas: the sandstone scarps that run from the north, swing round at Alnwick, to Rothbury and beyond, and the Cheviot Hills. A few other sites outside these areas are also included.

Maps referred to are essential Ordnance Survey sheets, mainly the Explorer and Outdoor Leisure Series. The sheet is numbered, and the general grid coordinates are added to denote the general areas of interest.

Ford Moss to Roughting Linn
(Outdoor Leisure 16; 96-98, 36-38)
A public footpath links the abandoned mine and settlement at Ford Moss (an area of special botanical interest) with Roughting Linn along the attractive sandstone ridge that has rock art and the Goatscrag Hill rock shelter (permission is needed from Roughting Linn farm to go up to this). The rock art site is the largest in northern England, close to a multivallate fort, and unsignposted.

Milfield
(NU 935 339)
The Maelmin Trail that begins near the Milfield Café is centred on a replica henge. Information boards reveal other histories.

Doddington
(Explorer 340; 00-03, 30-34)
There are many footpaths over Doddington Moor (start at the village, 999 325) running close to many sites with spectacular rock art, a small stone circle, a hillfort and other enclosures; many are marked on the map. Check with the map and farmers for access to anything not on a right of way.

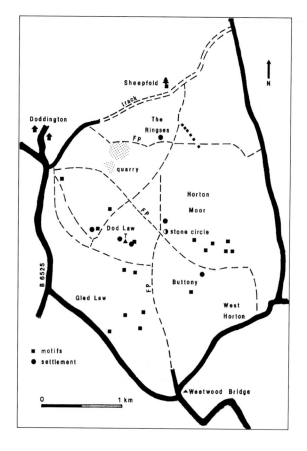

169 *The Doddington area.* I. Hewitt

Weetwood Moor

(Explorer 340; 00-04, 26-30. Main focus: NU 0215 2810)

Although the Fowberry sites (rock art, settlements, and burials) are restricted, there is access to the Weetwood cairn, rock art, cairns, and a good walk to the Coldmartin Lough area, with splendid views above Wooler. Reached by a minor road off the Wooler-Chatton road.

Chatton Park Hill

(Explorer 340; 07-08, 29-30. Main focus: NU 0757 2906)

Recently put into stewardship, the hill is one of the finest sites for rock art, the decorated floor of Ketley Crag, a ring work centred on decorated outcrop. Very good views. Pull up off the Belford-Chatton road.

Ros castle

(Explorer 340; 08-09, 25-26. NU 0798 2510)

Not a castle, but a hillfort (National Trust). Pull in off the Hepburn-A1 gated road (or use the Hepburn Forest car park). The climb to the top gives fantastic views of a wide, largely empty landscape with the coast visible. There is a pre-historic enclosure to the west on the scarp edge overlooking Hepburn Farm.

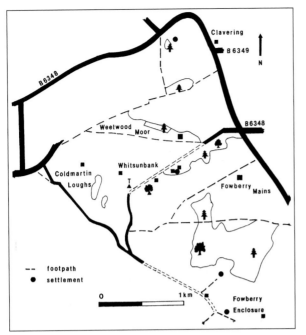

170 *Weetwood to Lilburn.*
I. Hewitt

Legend on map:
- - - footpath
● settlement

Labels on map 170:
Clavering
B 6349
B 6348
N
Weetwood Moor
Coldmartin Loughs
Whitsunbank
Fowberry Mains
0 ___ 1 km
Fowberry Enclosure

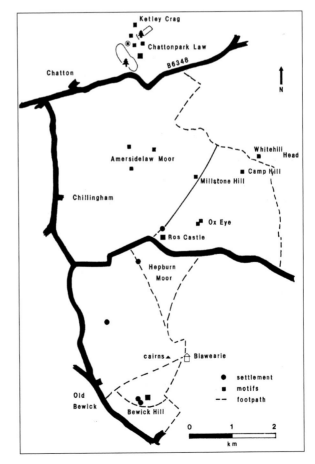

171 *Chatton Park Hill to
Old Bewick.* I. Hewitt

Labels on map 171:
Ketley Crag
Chattonpark Law
Chatton
B 6348
N
Amersidelaw Moor
Whitehill Head
Camp Hill
Millstone Hill
Chillingham
Ox Eye
Ros Castle
Hepburn Moor
cairns ▲ Blawearie
Old Bewick
Bewick Hill

Legend on map 171:
● settlement
■ motifs
- - - footpath
0   1   2
km

172 Old Bewick double hillfort

Old Bewick
(Explorer 332; 07-10, 21-24. Village: NU 066 215)
My favourite landscape, full of interest: two hillforts, excavated burial cairns and others. Overlooked by cairns on Hepburn Hill. Park at Old Bewick village (not much room). Public paths link good sites.

Beanley Moor/Hunterheugh/Titlington
(Explorer 332; 09-12, 16-19)
Under stewardship, with well-marked paths. A very large hillfort, The Ringses, standing stones and late settlements clearly defined. Hillfort in a wood. Much quarrying. At Hunterheugh there is rock art, cairns, settlements. Titlington Pike has a hillfort, cairns and standing stone. Varied terrain that can be difficult if you leave the paths.

Edlingham Valley
(Explorer 332; 10-14, 05-11)
Permission needed to visit Corby's Crags rock shelter and settlement, close to the Alnwick-Rothbury road. Caller Crags accessible by path near the junction with the A697. From here a path leads to the Snook Bank rock art sites, east of which are those at Millstone Burn and the Roman road.

173 *Beanley Moor from the south, with a focus on the Ringses (August 2002)*

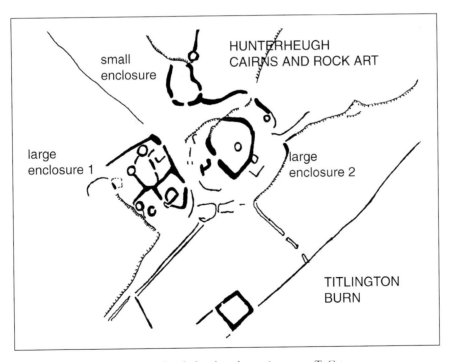

small
enclosure

HUNTERHEUGH
CAIRNS AND ROCK ART

large
enclosure 1

large
enclosure 2

TITLINGTON
BURN

174 *Hunterheugh, based on the gaspipe survey.* T. Gates

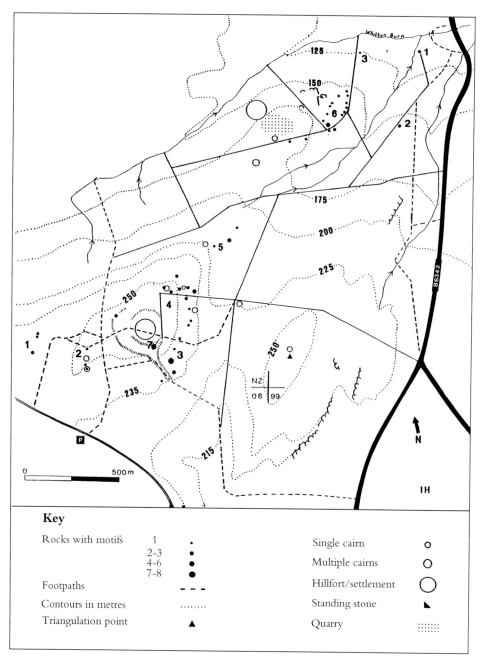

Key

Rocks with motifs	1	·	Single cairn	○
	2-3	⋮	Multiple cairns	◎
	4-6	●	Hillfort/settlement	◯
	7-8	●		
Footpaths	– – –		Standing stone	◣
Contours in metres	········			
Triangulation point	▲		Quarry	⠿

175 *Lordenshaw*. I. Hewitt

Callaly Castle
(Explorer 332; NU 06 097)
An accessible hillfort rising within a beautiful wood near the Whittingham road.

Lordenshaw and the Rothbury area
(Explorer 332, Outdoor Leisure 42 and Landranger Sheet 81; 03-07, 98-04)
A leaflet is obtainable from Northumberland National Park (at Rothbury and other information centres) on Lordenshaw, with its hillfort, cairns and rock art. A climb up the Simonside Hills gives good views, and some big cairns. To the north of the River Coquet, at Cartington, are cairns, rock art and fortified settlements.

Rochester
(Outdoor Leisure 42; 828-981)
Combine a visit to the Roman fort with the Redesdale centre and café (replica structures, named 'Brigantium').

Shaftoe/Bolam
(Outdoor Leisure 42; 05-09, 81-84)
The public path to Shaftoe Crags passes the Poind and his Man (large burial mound with standing stone). The sandstone scarp is of great interest, with dramatic formations. There is a settlement site, fortified, and rock art. At Bolam Lakes there is a good planned walk (car park, café) that runs close to sites from Mesolithic to Iron Age, although there is nothing to see.

Warden
(Outdoor Leisure 43. Hillfort is NY 9041 6786)
Near Hexham, public footpaths from the Boat Inn via Quality Cottages past Mesolithic sites and possible long barrow to the hilltop fort with its eastern appendages. Very good views. There are agricultural terraces.

Hadrian's Wall area
(Outdoor Leisure 43)
In the 'corridor', Milking Gap is an Iron Age settlement. South of Housesteads car park is a large barrow. North of the Wall are many sites of cord rig, standing stones and settlements, where access is very limited.

Coastal sites
Use *The Tides of Time* (Hardie 2000) as a guide to sites at Low Hauxley and Howick Camp.

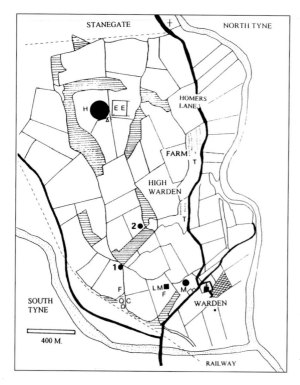

176 *Warden Hill, showing field boundaries and other features: EE eastern enclosures; F flint sites known previously; H hilltop enclosures; LM long mound; M motte; QC Quality Cottages; T terraces; 1 and 2 newly found Mesolithic sites.* Prepared by the author for the *Hexham Historian*

The Cheviot Hills

Yeavering and Humbleton Hill (Outdoor Leisure 16)

Northumberland National Park has produced a pamphlet on both, available to visitors. Both have good reconstructions in painting of the prehistoric landscape.

Apart from the major hillforts, there are sites like Monday Cleugh (NT 956 285) close to Humbleton, that can be reached; this is a fine hillfort on a cliff edge, with house sites inside. There is no official access, but it can be viewed from a public path.

College Valley (Outdoor Leisure 16)

There is a car park at the entrance to the valley, and one may walk through the rest or climb the slopes to Great and Little Hetha enclosures. There are many visible enclosures on the valley slopes and in the Elsdon Burn valley, superb field systems, and the remains of a stone circle on the valley floor.

Breamish/Ingram Valley (Outdoor Leisure 16; 95-04, 13-18)

This essential visit may begin at the Northumberland National Park Information Centre, from which maps and other information may be bought, or at Bulby's Wood car park (WCs). Many sites are reached by following posted routes. Further west along the valley the road is closed to cars at Greenside, but you may walk past Greaves Ash (a fine Iron Age village) just before Linhope, then walk to Linhope Spout and Standrop, where there are traces of houses and field systems.

177   Alwinton: Angryhaugh (meaning grassland by the river)

Alnham (Outdoor Leisure 16; 95-00, 10-13)
Alnham lies off a minor road from Alwinton to Whittingham. Ancient route-ways take you up to the hillfort, which lies in a wide area of cairns and settle-ments, including High Knowes.

Alwinton (Outdoor Leisure 16; 91-93, 06-09)
Alwinton gives access to many settlement sites and field systems, some along the ancient Clennel Street, but it is also the beginning of the road to a Danger Area used for military training.

Museums
The Museum of Antiquities, Newcastle, is part of the university campus at the Haymarket. There is a good range of prehistoric artefacts, but there are many more hidden away. Entry is free. There is Web access: www.ncl.nc.uk/antiquities. Text references: NUM.

The Border Museum, Berwick upon Tweed, houses artefacts, particularly pottery from the Milfield Plain and portable rock art from the Weetwood and Fowberry excavations. It is next door to the Barracks (paid entry).

Alnwick Castle Museum has many fine objects from the county and beyond, covering many periods of prehistory (paid entry).

Chillingham Castle houses the Berthele collection of flints and other objects from a great collection (paid entry).

Societies

Archaeological Societies continue to be the focus of much research, excavation and recording of our prehistory.

The old-established Society of Antiquaries of Newcastle upon Tyne publishes *Archaeologia Aeliana*.

The Northumberland Archaeological Group, consisting mostly of amateurs led by professionals, is one of the most active in the country, and regularly publishes *Northern Archaeology*, one of our finest journals for prehistory.

Taking on some of the roles of earlier research groups based on Berwick on Tweed is The Border Archaeological Society, which produces *The BAS Bulletin*.

All three societies have a programme of lectures and visits.

Northumberland is fortunate to have an Archaeology section at County Hall, Morpeth, with an excellent database. It produces an annual round-up of archaeological research that is invaluable to those who want to keep up with what is happening (see Bibliography).

The database will be available on the Internet from October, 2003 (log on to www.northumberland.gov.uk).

There are two major University Departments at Newcastle and Durham, and other universities occasionally base research projects on Northumberland.

CHRONOLOGY

Climate

Below is a simplified guide to period and climatic conditions in Britain in pre-historic times:

Middle Bronze Age to Roman (1100 BC-AD)	The climate deteriorates, becoming cold and wet
Late Neolithic to Middle Bronze Age (2500-1100 BC)	A stable climate, warm and dry
Early to Late Neolithic (4000-2500 BC)	Declining warmth; arable farming makes its entrance
Later Mesolithic (6000–4000 BC)	A warm and wet climate
Mesolithic warm and dry (7500-6000 BC)	A 'continental' type of climate:
Early Mesolithic (8300-7500 BC)	Increasing warmth

The main characteristics of prehistoric periods in Northumberland

The old division of prehistory was Stone, Bronze and Iron Age. Basically this is retained by archaeologists, but there are so many new sites and discoveries that all these divisions have been sub-divided, and go on being further sub-divided. One 'age' does not suddenly stop and another begin. However, it is helpful to see some general trends in the way people's use of the land has developed. Some sites that have clear examples of these characteristics are in italics.

Mesolithic (c.10000-4000 BC)
Meso-lithos means middle stone. A very small population was largely nomadic, harvesting the country without ploughing. Little is left in the record, as so much of their life was based on organic material, but scatters of distinctive stone tools (microliths) and flakes show where they camped or lived.

The earliest site is at *Howick (7800 BC)*, a cliff top by the sea. Many other sites are coastal, but others follow river valleys inland.

Neolithic (c4000-2100 BC)

Neo-lithos means new-stone. With it begins the introduction of arable farming and a gradual change from a wooded landscape to an open one with extensive pasture. The *Milfield Plain* is farmed.

Pigs and cattle are reared. Population increases with food production. There is a development from small households to settlements based on boundaries and hierarchies.

Pottery is introduced and develops in many forms, becoming increasingly ornate. New tools appear to support changes in land management and exploitation.

Very early houses are rarely found: one early fourth-century site is *Sandyford Quarry Field, Bolam*.

Monuments become prominent. Early long cairns give way to round cairns. Stone circles, standing stones, henges and pit alignments are constructed with communal links. Rock art spreads across landscapes and on monuments through to the Bronze Age (*Chatton Park, Roughting Linn, and Weetwood*).

Bronze Age (c.2100-700 BC)

So named because bronze is introduced for tools, ornaments and weapons. Stone artefact production continues, and new forms such as equal-barbed-and-tanged arrowheads are made.

The early phase marks the development of ornate pottery, especially Beakers and Food Vessels. These appear in burial cairns as well as in domestic contexts. Later burials use older mounds and bones are interred in rude domestic pots.

Exotic items of gold, jet and amber are produced. *Blawearie cairns, Chatton Sandyford, Kirkhaugh*.

Farming continues to develop. Lynchets, terraces and cord rig systems of fields are established. Enclosed and unenclosed settlements appear. *Houseledge, Standrop Rigg, Linhope* are among the earliest. Ring-groove houses are replaced by roundhouses with stone foundations.

Iron Age (c.700 BC-Roman)

So-named because iron is used to make weapons and tools, although bronze continues to be produced.

Hillfort-building intensifies, some occupying late Bronze Age sites. *Brough Law, Dod Law, Wether Hill, Warden, Alnham, Lordenshaw, Harehaugh*.

Settlements continue to have stone-based round houses, with field systems attached. *Fawdon Dean*.

There is little known pottery, and few known burial monuments.

A final perspective . . .

Mesolithic = *c.*6000 years; other prehistoric periods = *c.*4000 years: a total of *c.***10,000 years**.

The documented history of Britain from the Year of our Lord to the present is **2003 years**.

BIBLIOGRAPHY

Abbreviations

AA   *Archaeologia Aeliana* (Society of Antiquaries of Newcastle upon Tyne)
BAR   *British Archaeological Reports*
HBNC   *History of the Berwickshire Naturalists Club*
NA   *Northern Archaeology* (Bulletin of the Northumberland Archaeological
        Group, Newcastle)
PPS   *Proceedings of the Prehistoric Society*
PSAN   *Proceedings of the Society of Antiquaries of Newcastle*

General works on prehistory

Annable, R., 1987, *The later Prehistory of Northern England*, BAR Series 160 (i–iii)
Beckensall, S., 1999, *Prehistoric Rock Art in* Britain, Tempus
Bradley, R., 1978, *The Prehistoric Settlement of Britain*, Routledge
Bradley, R., 1984, *The social foundations of prehistoric Britain*, Longman
Bradley, R., 1988, *The significance of monuments*, Routledge
Burgess, C., 2001, *The Age of* Stonehenge, Phoenix
Chapman J.C., & Mytum, H. (eds), *Settlement in North Britain 1000 BC-AD 1000*, BAR 118, 103–48
Clarke, D.V., 1985, *Symbols of Power*, National Museum of Antiquities of Scotland, Edinburgh (HMSO)
Darvill, T., 1987, *Prehistoric Britain*, Batsford
Gibson, A., 2002, *Prehistoric Pottery in Britain & Ireland*, Tempus
Greene, K., 2002, *The history, principles and methods of modern archaeology*, Routledge
Higham, N., 1986, *The Northern Counties to AD 1000*, Longman
Malone, C., 2002, *Neolithic Britain and Ireland*, Tempus
Megaw, J., & Simpson, D., 1988, *Introduction to British Prehistory* (4th edition), Leicester University Press
Russell, M., 2002, *Monuments of the British Neolithic*, Tempus
Smith, C., 1992, *Late Stone Age Hunters of the British Isles*
Woodward, A., 2000, *British Barrows: A Matter of Life and Death*, Tempus

General works on Northumberland and related sites

Archaeology in Northumberland is a magazine produced annually by the Northumberland County Council, covering a variety of archaeological topics. Copies may be obtained free from County Hall, Morpeth.

Alnwick Catalogue, 1880. 'A descriptive catalogue of antiquities, chiefly British, at Alnwick Castle, Newcastle'

Beckensall, S., 1966, 'The excavation of Money Mound', *Sussex Archaeological Collections*, CV, 113-30

Beckensall, S., 2001(a), *Northumberland: the Power of Place*, Tempus

Beckensall, S., 2001(b), *Prehistoric Rock Art in Northumberland*, Tempus

Burgess, C.,1968, *Bronze Age Metalwork in Northern England*, Oriel Press, Newcastle

Burgess, C. & Miket, R. (eds), 'Settlement and economy in the third and second millennia', *BAR 33*

Dixon, D., *Upper Coquetdale*, Newcastle

Hardie, C. & Rushton, S., 2000, *The Tides of Time: Archaeology on the Northumberland Coast*, Northumberland County Council

Hogg, A.H.A., 1947, 'A new list of native sites in Northumberland', *PSNA*, 4, 11 (1946-50), 140-79.

Huntley, J.P. & Stallibrass, S.M., 1995, 'Plant and vertebrate remains from archaeological sites in northern England: data reviews and future directions', *Architectural and Arch. Society of Durham and Northumberland*

Miket, R. & Burgess, C. (eds), 1984, *Between and Beyond the Walls. Essays on the prehistory and history of North Britain in honour of G. Jobey*

Northumberland County History Committee, 1935, *A History of Northumberland*, volume XIV, pp.21-67. This is an early gazetteer of prehistoric sites

Specific references to Northumberland sites

Adams, M., 1996, 'Setting the Scene: the Mesolithic in Northern England', *NA* 13/14, 1-6

Allason Jones, L., 1983, 'Two axe-hammers from Northumberland' *NA* 3, 3-5

ASUD Annual Reports 1998-2000. The Breamish Valley Archaeology Project (Northumberland National Park)

Beckensall, S., 1976, 'The excavation of a rock shelter at Corby's Crags, Edlingham', *AA*, Ser. 5, 4, 11-16

Beckensall, S., 1998, 'The Archaeology of Warden Hill', *The Hexham Historian*, No. 8, p.2-19

Beckensall, S., Hewitt, I. & Hewitt, I., 1991, 'Prehistoric Rock Motifs Recently Recorded in Northumberland' *AA*, Ser. 5, 19, 1-6

Beckensall, S., 1995, 'Recent Discovery and Recording of Prehistoric Rock Motifs in the North' *NA*, 12, 9-34

Beckensall, S., 1996, 'Symbols on Stone: the State of the Art', *NA* 13/4, 139-46

Beckensall, S. & Frodsham, P., 1998, 'Questions of Chronology: the Case for Bronze Age Rock Art', *NA* 15/16, 51-69

Blood, K., 1995, 'Ros Castle Iron Age Hillfort, Chillingham' *NA* 12, 35-7

Bradley, R., 1996, 'Learning from Places – Topographical Analysis of North British Prehistoric Rock Art', *NA* 13/14, 87-100

Bradley, R., 1997, *Rock Art and the Prehistory of Atlantic Europe*, Routledge

Burgess, C.B., 1972, 'Goatscrag: a Bronze Age rock shelter cemetery in north Northumberland. With notes on other rock shelters and crag lines in the region' *AA*. Ser.3, 50, 15-70

Burgess, C.B. & Miket, R.F., 'A bronze axe from Elsdon, Northumberland, and the problem of Middle Bronze Age flanged axes' *AA*. Ser. 5, 2, 27-32

Burgess, C.B. & Miket, R.F., 1976, 'Three socketed axes from North-East England with notes on faceted and ribbed socketed axes', *AA*. Ser. 5, 5

Burgess, C., 1980, 'Excavations at Houseledge, Black Law, Northumberland, 1979, and their implications for earlier Bronze Age settlement in the Cheviots' *NA* 1, 5-13

Burgess, C., Owens, M. & Uribe de Kellett, A., 1981, 'The Ground and Polished Stone implements of North East England; A Preliminary Statement', *NA* 3, 6-12

Burgess, C., 1982, 'The Cartington Knife and the Double-Edged Knives of the Late Bronze Age', *NA*, 32-45

Burl, H.A. & Jones, N., 1972, 'The excavation of The Three Kings stone circle, Northumberland', *AA* Ser. 4, 50, 1-14

Charlton, B. & Day, J., 1978, 'Excavation and field survey in Upper Redesdale', *AA* Ser. 5, 61-86

Charlton, B., 1982, 'A Bronze Age Settlement on Todlaw Pike, Otterburn', *NA* 3-5

Collingwood, E.F. & Cowen, J.D., 1946, 'A prehistoric grave at West Lilburn', *AA* Ser. 4, 24, 207-29

Collingwood, E.F., 1948, 'A prehistoric grave at Haugh Head Wooler', *AA* Ser. 4, 26, 47-54

Collingwood, E.F. & Jobey, G., 1961, 'A food vessel burial at West Lilburn', *AA* Ser. 4, 37, 3-80

Cowley, D. & O'Brien, C., 1990, 'Gunner Peak East, Barrasford, Northumberland', *NA* 10, 15-18

Cowley, D., 'Some Burnt mounds in mid-Northumberland', *AA*, Ser. 5, 19, 119-21

Craw, J.H., 1934, 'Neolithic cairns in Northumberland and the Duddo stone circle', *HBNC* 28 (for 1932-4), 80, 84-6

Davies, J., 1983, 'The Mesolithic Sites of Northumberland', *NA* 4(11), 18-24

Davies, J. & Davidson, J., 1988, 'A survey of Bolam and Shaftoe area, Northumberland', *NA* 9, 57-96

Davies, J., 1995, 'Bolam and Shaftoe: a Second Survey', *NA* 12, 51-77

English Heritage, 2002, Reports on Archaeological Field Investigations by English Heritage in the Northumberland National Park. Hillfort surveys of Castle Hill, Alnham, Glead's Cleugh, Great Hetha, Yeavering Bell, Humbleton Hill, West Hill, Fawcett Shank, Hethpool Bell, Mid Hill, Staw Hill, Ring Chesters, and St Gregory's Hill. These are all individual volumes, published in York

Ferrell, G., 1990, 'A re-assessment of the Prehistoric Pottery from the 1952-62. Excavations at Yeavering', *AA* Ser. 5, 17

Frodsham, P. (ed.), 1996, 'Neolithic Studies in No Man's Land', *NA* 13/14

Frodsham, P., 1996, 'Spirals in Time: Morwick Mill and the Spiral Motif in the British Neolithic', *NA* 13/14, 101-38

Frodsham, P., 1999, 'Forgetting Gefrin: Elements of the Past in the Past at Yeavering', *NA* 17/18, 191-207

Frodsham, P., 2000, 'Worlds Without Ends. Towards a new prehistory for central Britain' in Harding, J. & Johnson, R. (eds), *Northern Pasts: Interpretation of the Later Prehistory of Northern England and Southern Scotland*, *BAR* British Series 302, Oxford

Frodsham, P., forthcoming, 'Archaeology in the Northumberland National Park', *CBA*, York

Frodsham, P., Topping, P. & Cowley, D. (eds), 1999, '"We were always chasing Time": papers presented to Keith Blood', *NA* 17/18

Gates, T., 1982, 'A long cairn on Dod Hill, Ilderton, Northumberland', *AA* 5, Vol. 10, 210-11

Gates, T. & O'Brien, C., 1988, 'Cropmarks at Milfield and New Bewick and the recognition of Grubenhauser in Northumberland', *AA* Ser. 5, 16, 1-10

Gibson, A., 1981, 'Some Perforated Stone Artefacts from Northumberland and Durham', *NA* 2, 3-7

Greenwell, W. & Rolleston, G., 1877, *British Barrows*, Clarendon Press, Oxford

Harding, A., 1981, 'Excavations in the Prehistoric Ritual Complex near Milfield, Northumberland', *PPS* 47, 87-135

Hewitt, I., 1991, 'Prehistoric decorated stones: mobiliary examples', *NA* 11, 51-6

Hewitt, I., 1995, 'Prehistoric Artefacts from North Northumberland Forests: The Berthele Collection', *NA* 12, 3-8

Hewitt, I. & Beckensall, S., 1996, 'The Excavation of Cairns at Blawearie, Old Bewick, Northumberland', *PPS* Vol. 62, 255-74

Hogg, A.H.A. & N., 1956, 'Doddington and Horton Moors', *AA* Ser. 4, 34, 142-9

Hogg, A.H.A., 1956, 'Further Excavations at Ingram Hill', *AA* Ser. 4, 34, 150-60

Holbrook, N., 1988, 'The settlement at Chester House, Northumberland', *AA* Ser. 5, 16, 47-60

Hope-Taylor, B., 1977, 'Yeavering: an Anglo-British centre of early Northumbria', *Department of the Environment Archaeological Reports* 7, (HMSO)

Jarratt, M.G. & Evans, D.A., 1986, 'Excavations of Two Palisaded Enclosures at West Whelpington, Northumberland', *AA* Ser. 5, 17, 117-40

Jobey, G., 1957, 'Excavations at the native settlement, Gubeon Cottage, Northumberland', *AA* Ser. 4, 35, 163-79

Jobey, G., 1959, 'Excavations at the native settlement at Huckoe, Northumberland', *AA* Ser. 4, 217-78

Jobey, G., 1962, 'A note on scooped enclosures in Northumberland', *AA* Ser. 4, 40, 47-58

Jobey, G., 1965, 'An early bronze age burial at Reaverhill Farm, Barrasford, Northumberland', *AA* Ser. 4, 43, 65-76

Jobey, G., 1965, 'Hillforts and settlements in Northumberland', *AA* Ser. 4, 43, 21-64

Jobey, G., 1966, 'Excavations on palisaded settlements and cairnfields at Alnham, Northumberland', *AA* Ser. 4, 44, 5-48

Jobey, G., 1968, 'Excavations of cairns at Chatton Sandyford, Northumberland', *AA* Ser. 4, 46, 5-50

Jobey, G., 1970, 'An Iron Age settlement and homestead at Burradon, Northumberland', *AA* Ser. 4, 51-96

Jobey, G., 1971, 'Excavations at Brough Law and Ingram Hill', *AA* Ser. 4, 49, 71-93

Jobey, G., 1972, 'Notes on additional early settlements in Northumberland', *AA* Ser. 4, 50, 71-80

Jobey, G., 1973, 'A native settlement at Hartburn and the Devil's Causeway', *AA* Ser. 4, 1, 11-54

Jobey, G. & Newman, T.G., 1975, 'A collared urn cremation at Howick, Northumberland', *AA* Ser. 5, 3, 1-16

Jobey, G., 1977, 'Iron Age and later farmsteads on Belling Law, Northumberland', *AA* Ser. 5, 5, 1-38

Jobey, G., 1977, 'A Food Vessel burial on Dour Hill, Byrness, Northumberland', *AA* Ser. 5, 204-7

Jobey, G., 1978, 'Iron Age and Romano-British settlements on Kennel Hall Knowe, North Tynedale, Northumberland' *AA* Ser. 5, 1-28

Jobey, G., 1978, 'A Beaker burial from Altonside, Haydon Bridge, Northumberland', *AA* Ser. 5, 6, 173-4

Jobey, G., 1981, 'Groups of small cairns and the excavation of a cairnfield on Millstone Hill, Northumberland', *AA* Ser. 5, 9, 23-44

Jobey, G., 1983, 'Excavation of an unenclosed settlement on Standrop Rigg, Northumberland, and some problems related to similar settlements between Tyne and Forth', *AA* Ser. 5, 11, 1-22

Jobey, G., 1988, 'Gowanburn River camp: an Iron Age Romano-British and more recent settlement in North Tyneside, Northumberland', *AA* Ser. 5, 16, 11-28

Johnston, R. & Pollard, J., 1999, 'Survey and excavation at Kellah Burn', *Archaeology in Northumberland*, 22-3, Northumberland County Council

Maddison, M. & Sellers, P., 1990, 'A survey of Doddington and Horton Moors, Northumberland', *NA* 10, 29-75

McCord, N., 1968, 'Notes on air reconnaissance in Northumberland and Durham', *AA* Ser. 4, 46, 51-8

McCord, N. & Jobey, G., 1971, 'Notes on air reconnaissance in Northumberland and Durham 2', *AA* Ser. 4, 49, 119-30

McOmish, D., 1999, 'Wether Hill and Cheviots Hillforts', *NA* Vol. 17/18, 113-21

Miket, R., 1974, 'Excavation at Kirkhill, West Hepple, 1972', *AA* Ser. 5, 2, 153-88

Miket, R., 1976, 'The evidence for Neolithic activity in the Milfield Basin, Northumberland' in Burgess, C. & Miket, R. (eds), *Settlement and Economy in the Third and Second Millennium BC,* Oxford: British Archaeological reports 33, 113-33

Miket, R., 1985, 'Ritual Enclosures on Whitton Hill, Northumberland', *PPS* 51, 137-48

Moffat, J.G., 1885, 'Prehistoric grave from the Lilburn Hill Farm, on the Lilburn Tower Estate', *AA* Ser. 2, 10, 220-2

Monaghan, J.M., 1994, 'An unenclosed Bronze Age House Site in Lookout Plantation, Northumberland', *AA* Ser. 5, 22, 29-42

Newbigin, N., 1935, 'Excavations of a long and a round cairn on Bellshiel Law, Redesdale', *AA* Ser. 4, 13, 293-309

Newbigin, N., 1941, 'A collection of prehistoric material from Hebburn Moor, Northumberland', *AA* Ser. 4, 19, 104-16

Newman, T.G., 1976, 'The jet necklace from Kyloe, Northumberland', *AA* Ser. 5, 4. 177-82

Newman, T.G., 1977, 'Two Early Bronze Age cist burials in Northumberland', *AA* Ser. 5, 39-46

Newman, T.G. & Miket, R., 'A dagger grave at Allerwash, Newbrough, Northumberland', *AA* Ser. 5, 87-96

Page, H. & Turner-Walker, G., 1991, 'The Bronze Age Dagger from Reaverhill Farm, Barrasford', *AA* Ser. 5, 1991, 127-30

Prothero, H., 1998, 'A Survey of Kirkwhelpington and Ridsdale Areas, Northumberland', *NA* 15/16, 109-44

Smith, C., 1990, 'Excavations at Dod Law West hillfort, Northumberland', *NA* 9 (1998-9), 1-55 (see also under Tolan-Smith)

Stopford, J. *et al.*, 1985, 'Two cemeteries of the second millennium BC in Northumberland', AA Ser. 5, 117-32

Stallibrass, S. & Huntley, J., 1996, 'Slim evidence: A Review of the Faunal and Botanic Data from the Neolithic of Northern England', *NA* 13/14, 35-42

Tait, T., 1965, *Beakers from Northumberland*, Newcastle

Tait, T., 1968, 'Neolithic Pottery from Northumberland', *AA* Ser. 4, 46, 275-81

Tate G., 1862, 'On the old Celtic town at Greaves Ash near Linhope, Northumberland with an account of diggings recently made into this and other ancient remains in the valley of Breamish', *History of the Berwick Naturalist's Field Club 4*, 293-316

Tipping, R., 1992, 'The determination of cause in the generation of major prehistoric valley fills in the Cheviot Hills, Anglo-Scottish border' in Needham, S. & Macklin, M.C. (eds), *Alluvial archaeology in Britain*, Oxbow monograph 27

Tipping, R., 1996, 'The Neolithic landscapes of the Cheviot Hills and Hinterland: Palaeoenvironmental Evidence', *NA* 13/14, 17-34

Tolan-Smith, C., 1996, 'Landscape Archaeology in Tynedale', *Department of Archaeology, University of Newcastle upon Tyne* (see also under Smith, C.)

Tolan-Smith, C., 1996, 'The Mesolithic/Neolithic Transition in the Lower Tyne valley: a landscape approach', *NA* 13/14, 7-16

Topping P., 1982, 'The Prehistoric Field Systems of the College Valley, North Northumberland', *NA* 3, 3-9

Topping, P., 1983, 'Observations on the stratigraphy of Early Agricultural Remains in the Kirknewton area of the North East Cheviots', *NA* 4, 21-31

Topping, P., 1989, 'The Linhope Burn Excavations, Northumberland, 1989. Interim Report', *NA* 8, 29-34

Topping, P. (ed.) 1989, 'Early Cultivation in Northumberland and the Borders', *PPS* 55, 161-79

Topping, P., 1990, 'A survey of north Black Hagg hillfort, Northumberland (NT 8836 2505)', *NA* 10, 27-8

Topping, P., 1991, 'The excavation of an unenclosed settlement, field system and cord rig cultivation at Linhope Burn, Northumberland', *NA* 11, 1-42

Topping, P., 1993, 'Lordenshaws Hillfort and its environs', *AA* Ser.5. (1993), 15-28

Topping, P. (ed.), 1997, 'Different Realities: the Neolithic in the Northumberland Cheviots' in *Neolithic Landscapes*, Oxbow Monograph 86

Topping, P., 1998, 'The Excavation of Burnt Mounds at Titlington Mount, North Northumberland, 1992-3', *NA* 15/16, 3-26

Topping P., 1999, 'A Survey of Little Hetha Hillfort, Northumberland', *NA* 17/18, 123-8

Turner, R.C., 'A Late Neolithic site at High House, Matfen', *AA* Ser. 5, 17, 215

Twohig, E., 1988, 'The rock carvings at Roughting Linn, Northumberland', *AA* Ser. 5, 16, 37-46

Tyne and Wear Archaeology Unit and Northumberland County Council Archaeology and Building Conservation Team, 1994, *An Archaeological Survey of the Carr–Ellison Estate at Beanley, Northumberland*, Northumberland C.C.

Waddington, C., 1996, 'The 1995 Excavation on the Coupland Enclosure and Associated "Droveways" in the Milfield Plain, Northumberland', *Universities of Durham and Newcastle upon Tyne Archaeological Reports for 1995*, 9-15

Waddington, C., 1996, 'Putting Rock Art to Use. A model of Early Neolithic Transhumance in North Northumberland', *NA* 13/14, 147-78

Waddington, C., 1997, 'Notes: Coupland: The Earliest Henge-type monument in Britain', *AA* Ser. 5, 25, 144-5

Waddington, C., 1997, 'A review of "Pit Alignments" and a tentative interpretation of the Milfield complex, *Durham Archaeological Journal* 13, 21-3

Waddington, C., 1998, 'Cup and ring marks in context', *Cambridge Archaeological Journal*, Vol. 8, No. 1

Waddington, C. & Davies, J., 1998, 'The excavation of an Early Neolithic Settlement and an Adjacent Cairn at Sandyford Quarry Field: An Interim Report', *NA* 15/16, 45-50

Waddington, C., Blood, K., & Crow, J., 1998, 'Survey and excavation at Harehaugh Hillfort and possible Neolithic Enclosure', *NA* Vol. 15/16, 87-108

Waddington, C., 1998, 'Humbleton Hill Hillfort Survey', *NA* 15/16, 71-81

Waddington, C., 1999, 'A landscape archaeological study of the Mesolithic-Neolithic in the Milfield Basin', *BAR* 291

Waddington, C., 2002, 'Breaking out of the morphological straitjacket: early Neolithic enclosures in northern Britain', *Durham Arch. Journal* Vol. 16, 1-14

Waddington, C. & John Davies, with contributions by Jacqui Huntley and Paul Hindmarch, 2002, 'An Early Neolithic settlement and Late Bronze Age Burial Cairn near Bolam Lake, Northumberland: fieldwalking, excavation and reconstruction', *AA* Ser. 5, 30, 1-47

Welfare, A., 1986, 'The Greenlee Lough (Northumberland) Palimpsest; an Interim Report on the 1985 Season', *NA* 7 (11), 35-45

Van Hoek, M., 1991, 'The Rock Art at Millstone Burn, Northumberland', *AA* Ser. 5, 19

INDEX OF SITES

Illustrations are in **bold**